Praise for *Off the Hook*

"Nancy Besonen's weekly columns in the *L'Anse Sentinel* always made me smile, or chuckle and, quite often, even snort with mirth. Besonen connects so well with our quirky Yooper culture and its priorities. Her perspective of our everyday lives is hilarious and reminiscent of the late Erma Bombeck."

Terri Martin, author and U.P. Notable Book Award recipient

"A veteran journalist, Nancy Besonen has a wonderful gift for sweet and tangy, humorous writing and storytelling. She uses visual, nuanced language to paint portraits of Michigan's Upper Peninsula's people, places and events, infusing culture, history and geography. Her colorful tales, filled with wit, action, twists and turns, are a must read for those in Michigan (and beyond), as she inspires us all to think about our own life journeys."

Martha Bloomfield,
award-winning author, oral historian, artist and poet

"Besonen, a gifted journalist who moved north from Chicago for the fishing and brought with her a deep sensibility for the U.P, both teaches and inspires. This is true nonfiction at its best, both wit and investigative journalism. I am glad she collects it here."

Mack Hassler, former professor of English, Kent State University

Off the Hook

Off-Beat Reporter's Tales
from Michigan's U.P.

Nancy Besonen

Modern History Press

Ann Arbor, MI

ISBN 978-1-61599-748-0 paperback
ISBN 978-1-61599-749-7 hardcover
ISBN 978-1-61599-750-3 eBook

Modern History Press info@ModernHistoryPress.com
5145 Pontiac Trail   www.ModernHistoryPress.com
Ann Arbor, MI 48105 Tollfree 888-761-6268

Distributed by INGRAM Book Group (USA/CAN/EU/AU)

Thank God

and the *L'Anse Sentinel*

Contents

Watton, Michigan and Local Area

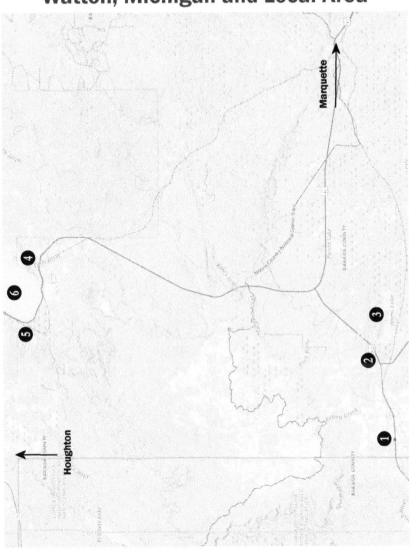

1. Watton
2. Covington
3. Worm Lake
4. L'Anse
5. Baraga
6. Keweenaw Bay

Michigan's Upper Peninsula

1. HOOK, LINE & SINK HER

No B-Word on the Boat

I was minding my own business at the Baraga County Lake Trout Festival which, me being a reporter, means I was minding everyone else's business when I was suddenly cast into darkness.

It was Ed Fugenschuh. He'd stepped between me and the sun, and the planet didn't stand a chance. Ed looked down at me, big as a mountain and rough as Lake Superior in a stiff northeast wind, and rumbled, "I want you to research somethin'."

My first thought was, controversy! I am not a huge fan of controversy. My personal motto is, "Got a problem? Call a cop." And I was just about to suggest Officer Pat Butler, who is great with kids and probably fishermen too and even gives out stickers, when Ed said, "Bananas on a boat."

I was still in the dark but now I was beaming, because this was just the type of story I was born to write.

Putting pen to notepad, I took down the facts. Ed's team was enjoying a great start in the festival's Keweenaw Classic Fishing Tournament. They'd boated a nine-pound salmon, then a five pounder. Then someone ate a banana and the fish quit biting.

"What is it with bananas on boats?" Ed asked.

He'd also heard that when another fisherman in the tournament brought out a piece of banana bread, he was forced to throw it overboard.

If there is one thing that sets this reporter's pen on fire, it is the shameful waste of baked goods, especially if they are buttered. Snapping my notepad closed, I promised Ed I would get to the bottom of this, using every available resource known to mankind.

That's right. I Googled it.

After having spent several hours on the computer, I am confident in reporting there's not much new on Facebook. Also, there is some substance to the popular belief that bananas have no place on fishing boats.

The theory dates all the way back to Caribbean trade in the 1700s. Sailboats had to hurry to deliver bananas before their expiration date. Sailors liked to troll during deliveries, and banana boats moved too fast for the fish to catch up to the bait.

Another theory holds that tropical spiders and snakes sometimes boarded with the bananas, which made it tough for the sailors to focus on their fishing. Still another notes that when boats carrying bananas sunk, all that was left behind was floating fruit, which was very incriminating to bananas in general.

Fish apparently don't like the smell of bananas, which can transfer from hand to lure. On an interesting side note, I used to have a licorice-scented rubber frog in my tackle box when I was a kid. As an attractant it ranked right up there with bananas, but it made my box smell better.

Finally, there are charter boat captains who absolutely prohibit the use of Banana Boat sunscreen products on their boats, just because they include the b-word. One won't even allow Fruit of the Loom underwear on his boat because of the bananas on the labels, and gives great big wedgies to offenders.

Ed, I hope this answers your question. Next time, how about a piece on licorice-scented frogs?

Living with SAD

I huddled in a corner of the doctor's office, thumbing a copy of *In-Fisherman* while jigging my tea bag in my cup. When the receptionist called my name, I tied off the string to the handle, handed it to her, and said, "Watch this—I think I felt a tap!"

I followed the nurse to an exam room, stumbling a bit when my ice grips snagged on the carpeting. Frowning down at my feet, she advised me to lose the hardware before stepping onto her scale.

"You're up a few pounds," she noted.

"It's the propane for my heater," I explained, opening my coat to reveal a spare tank tucked into a pocket. "I'm also wearing a few extra layers. Traps the warmth, you know."

She eyed my streaked coat sleeves, nudged a box of tissues in my direction, and said we'd forego the blood pressure check this time. Then turning to the laptop on her desk, she flipped it open and got busy typing.

"Marking anything?" I asked, nodding at the screen.

"Just the facts," she sighed. "Now, what can we do for you today?"

"I've got the SAD," I said.

"Seasonal Affective Disorder?" she asked.

"No, Seasonal Angling Disorder!"

It happens every year around this time, if I'm lucky, that is. Winter sets in, Lake Superior's Keweenaw Bay ices over, and I can't summon the energy to do anything but fish.

On cleaning days, the house gets a lick and a promise I have no intention of keeping. The dishes still get done, but only because I need the sink to clean my fish. I have a chronic case of hat head, and can't sleep at night thinking of the ones that got away.

On the bright side, the cat can't get enough of me.

The problem with Seasonal Angling Disorder is, nobody truly understands the condition unless they've lived it. That is why I gravitate at every opportunity to the colony—I mean, "ice fishing community"—on Keweenaw Bay.

I was there this past Sunday (and Thursday, Friday, and Saturday) when I ran into another SAD subject with the same symptoms. He had arrived at daylight, just slightly before me. His case was clearly more advanced.

His tent was already out on the ice, and he was holding a rusty double-bladed ax that he uses for reopening his iced-over fishing hole. Some people might have become alarmed and fled the scene. I sensed a kindred spirit and settled in for a visit.

We talked animatedly about everything, as long as it had to do with fishing: how many we've caught this season, how big, how deep, what time of day, etc. We formed a regular bond, though we didn't bother exchanging names because it just wasn't relevant.

That is how we SAD people roll, at least until spring, and then a few of us float because some people don't know when to stop. I haven't taken the plunge yet, but I did fish a half mile out on Keweenaw Bay one day, and returned the next to find waves crashing against the shore.

It's because I have a sickness. See you out on the ice! Right after I get my prescription filled at the local bait shop.

Tallest Tale of All

Around this time every year, I used to leave my writing to my readers.

Some would say it was my finest work.

It was my annual Fish Tales contest! It began on Memorial Day with a dare: write and send me a fish tale so preposterous, you hesitate to waste postage on it. Then sit back and wait to see if you win a fabulous prize and have your story printed in the Labor Day issue of your hometown newspaper.

My fabulous prizes ranged from beer can bobbers to ugly t-shirts to cool keychains shaped like a fishing reel. People did not enter the Fish Tales contest for personal profit. They did it for the glory of bragging rights as the biggest fish tale spinner in Baraga County. And maybe a cool keychain, too.

Well, Labor Day came and went and we all missed the boat. But the Fish Tales contest will return someday, and with that in mind, I'd like to bait my readers with the best tale ever told. "It's a true story told to me by Gen Van Loo that I like to call: Don't Worry, Be Happy."

Don Van Loo of Watton was bigger than life, and full of fun and trouble. His wife, Gen, had a heart as big as her husband, and was an avid collector of recipes and thrift store finds. Gen's thrill at sharing her treasures and homemade cookies made every visit sweet.

Don loved to share jokes and funny stories. One of his favorites was about a child sitting beside him in church one day, wiggling a loose tooth. Don leaned in and said, "Let me help you out there, buddy," and deftly plucked a present for the Tooth Fairy.

He was immediately rewarded with a gap-toothed smile. Then all *h*— (not heaven) broke loose as the parents rained down grief on their now-howling child. The child was supposed to keep his smile fully intact for family photos later in the day. So Don left church a little early.

Don also loved Fish Tales, and I could always count on him for a highly entertaining entry. Our secret panel of judges also appreciated his work, and over the years he managed to squeeze two grand prizes out of my tight fist. One, my Big Mouth Billy Bass, was a classic.

Billy was a plastic largemouth bass, and so much more. The obnoxious thing was battery-operated, and mounted on a plaque.

When you pressed a red button underneath the fish, it sang "Don't Worry, Be Happy" while flapping its head and tail to the beat.

Don had a wall of fame in his house that held trophy deer mounts, a bear skin and right in the middle of it all, his goofy old Big Mouth Billy Bass. He'd press Billy's button for company. He'd press it for Gen. He'd press it for the dog. Don couldn't get enough of Big Mouth Billy Bass.

We lost a great storyteller and friend when Don died several years ago. Family and friends rallied around Gen, who was so strong, and Don might have added a little support too, based on the final performance of his Big Mouth Billy Bass.

It happened three or four months after Don had died. Gen said she was puttering around the kitchen one day when the bass suddenly burst into the song: "Don't Worry, Be Happy."

She ignored it at first, figuring the batteries must have misfired in their old age. Then the bass repeated the short concert. Gen crossed the room, switched the button on the back of the plaque to *off*, and shut down Billy.

A couple of days later, the fish started singing again. This time Gen hollered, "C'mon, Don!" and took the blasted thing down from the wall. She turned it over to remove the batteries and silence Big Mouth Billy Bass for good.

But there were no batteries in the fish.

Why I Like Pike

I like pike.

Well, that's weeded out about 70 percent of my fellow fishermen. If you listen closely, you can almost hear their grumbles of "Bah! Snakes and hammer handles! Not to mention those stinkin' Y bones!"

Every oath is true of course, and I utter them several times a summer myself. But you've got to admire a creature that boasts a vicious strike, a head lined with teeth and the ability to thoroughly slime its captor. It's more than a fish. It's an alien.

Here in the U.P., northern pike can grow as long as a short fisherman, but are considerably lighter. They're found in the Great Lakes and in many of the lesser ones, too. So why is their following so small?

Yoopers already have to put up with too much snow, too many bugs and too little summer, but they have a choice when it comes to fishing. Most set their hooks for fish that don't try to bite them back, like that U.P. delicacy, brook trout.

Brook trout thrive in creeks that barely crest a high-top sneaker, and rivers so turbulent you wonder how the rocks survive. They hit lightly on worms, and aren't so much hooked as simply flipped out of the water and onto a grassy bank.

I shouldn't say "simply" because I've so far failed miserably at the technique, but the point is, you'd hardly even have to touch a brookie to catch one. Bugs and brush take their toll on brook trout fishermen, but for the most part, the fish are only too kind.

Pike taste great, too, and that's about the extent of their similarity to trout. If you're casting a spoon, spinner, or surface plug, a passing pike will hit it like a freight train. With a splash or a big swirl, your lure is rudely yanked in the opposite direction. You yank back, and a pike fight is on!

You seldom have to set the hook because pike inhale it, burying every barb deep in their bony mouths. They drag your line through the muckiest weed beds and toughest lily pads, then dive beneath the boat. As a final insult, they toss and roll in the net until it's a hopeless tangle of muck, line, fish, and slime.

Congratulations! You have a northern pike.

If you're not careful about handling it, you will have a doctor bill, too. A pike in the net would like nothing better than to add a couple of your digits to the perch already crowding its belly. Long-nose pliers work best for safely extracting what's left of your lure from the fish.

A good fight will chip paint off a spinner, kink a leader, and shred a bucktail. That's why you don't see pike fishermen displaying their lures on vests, or toting them around in see-through tackle boxes. What's left of their artillery is just too blamed ugly for a visual.

If catch and release is not the goal, then cleaning your pike is the next hurdle you'll face. Its tight scales will travel farther than you did to catch the fish. If your kitchen, like mine, doubles as a cleaning shack, the evidence will continue to surface long after the dirty deed is done.

I learned how to skin a pike long ago, which created a new problem. Soon Dad and then everyone else started handing the job over to me because I could do it more efficiently. You'll have to work

Teach a boy to fish and you'll wind up with sand in your camera, but a smile that's worth a lens that now grates a little.

that out for yourself. Don't bring me your fish.

I can get most of the major bones out, like the fin bone, the tail bone, and the head bone, but after that it's anybody's guess. Leftover "Y" bones are the most treacherous; upon entering your mouth they head straight for your palate, a final hit by a truly fighting fish.

They fight dirty, they try to bite you, they ruin your tackle and mess up your kitchen. So why do I like pike?

I like the fact they will hit on virtually anything that moves, and require little finesse on the part of the angler. Presentation? No sweat. I've watched a Dardevle spoon slide down a tall weed into the jaws of a pike, and I've bounced a spinner off the side of a docked boat into a waiting pike's gullet.

I've bounced my share of lures inside docked boats, too, but apparently the owners didn't have any pike onboard.

Most of the pike I catch aren't big enough to bring home, but hooking into even a 24-inch fish can really rattle me. They shatter that peaceful kind of feeling you get from bobbing along in a rowboat on a quiet lake, and the fight is never over until the last bite is done.

Ask Miss Demeanor

During the dog days of summer, it is easy for we fishermen to get a bit casual about our personal appearances and social graces. Our boats that gleamed on opening day now look like full recycling bins. We need hook removers to extract lures from our tangled tackle boxes. We leave live bait on our hooks between outings. Our biggest catch for July was the family cat.

For the reasons above and many more, which are just too rude to mention, it's time for another visit with our fishing manners expert, Miss Demeanor!

Q: Miss Demeanor, my wife is threatening that if I don't wash my lucky t-shirt, the one with the rip in its back and fish gut stains on the front, she will leave me for someone who plays tennis. Please advise.

A: Reader Dearest, it stands to reason that if you let her wash the shirt, you will never catch another fish for as long as you live. Miss Demeanor feels that compromise is the key to a good relationship. If you can't compromise your wife's standards, you must compromise your own.

Wear that lucky t-shirt only while fishing. If it gets a bit too "lucky," try this trick that cuts Miss Demeanor's laundering time in half: turn it inside out for another season of use!

Q: Hey, Miss D. If I take my girlfriend fishing, shouldn't she clean the fish?

A: Only if you are serious about the relationship, and want to start conditioning her for married life.

Q: Miss Demeanor, when I eat fish in a restaurant, I never know where to put the bones. What is the polite thing to do?

A: Order the beef. Sorry, Reader Dearest! The cheap shots are always the easiest. If the restaurant is fancy, you may discreetly hide them in your napkin by pretending to cough into it after every bony bite. Just don't use it for sneezing later in the meal, or you'll come up looking like you kissed a quill pig.

If the restaurant isn't fancy, simply stick the bones on the side of your plate, same as you do at home. Just remember to leave a generous tip for the poor waitress whom you are about to pierce.

Q: Miss Demeanor, my husband has been missing since opening day. When can I have him legally declared MIA, and get on with my life?

A: Refer to your Michigan DNR fishing guide, and allow three days after the season ends for him to find his way back home. Brook trout fishermen will require seven days to extract themselves from heavy brush. Best of luck.

If you find yourself unattached and attracted to gentlemen who favor camouflage or blaze orange, be sure to pick up a Michigan DNR hunting guide in the fall. Same reason.

Q: Miss Demeanor, what do you do if you're fishing with a friend who is catching all the fish, and he keeps razzing you with, "Your turn next!" or "You're up, bud!"

A: Reader Dearest, Miss Demeanor has been in this very situation more times than she cares to admit, and it does test one sorely. When you've reached your limit and your friend's back is turned as he reels yet another one in, select the stoutest rod in the boat and administer a firm whack between his ears, proclaiming, "There's a hit for ya'!"

The verbal abuse and, quite possibly the unrewarding fishing trip, should end soon after.

Q: Miss Demeanor, I have seen your boat. I know what your tackle box looks like, and I've had the rotten luck of running into you when you're doing a load of your "lucky" t-shirts at the Laundromat. My question is, how do you get off advising other people about social graces?

A: I always remember to say please and thank you. In the course of only five years, I earned a four-year college degree. The cat has almost healed. I AM Miss Demeanor!

Fish Camp Follies

Dear Friends,

Greetings from Fish Camp! I would write you all a postcard, but this is a whole lot cheaper. Besides, the Wampum Shop in Mercer is fresh out of the ones picturing a monster bass balanced on a wooden rowboat.

In case you did not get my postcard last year, Fish Camp is a time-honored tradition in which great minds gather for a week of fishing in northern Wisconsin.

HAHAHAHAHA!

Ouch! That raucous laughter hurts my great mind, which is still recovering from a work titled "Busch Light." The reason for my irreverent outburst is, the aforementioned minds belong to Slick (aka my brother, Mark), me, our two teenage sons, and The Boys.

The Boys are a gang from Chicago's South Side who grew up on the wrong side of the tracks, no matter which side they lived on. Slick, Mard, J.K. and LeGear shared playgrounds and pool halls, John Wayne movies, and Dean Martin tunes. They, like their heroes, are classics.

The youngsters, Mike and Sam, are The Boys in training. One strums a guitar and the other plays CDs. One is dark-haired, the other fair. Both fish with their shirts off and their motor at full throttle, laughing wildly as lures dangling over the side of their boat dance across the sparkling lake.

I am HB, an acronym for a very rude title I earned by occasionally swiping a dust rag around the cabin. I am also Designated Driver, World's Worst Pool Player and the misguided person who once brought a bag of apples to Fish Camp.

"Who brought these?" Slick growled. "Is this so we don't get the kids taken away? Get these things offa' the table!"

And so forth. In keeping with time-honored tradition, Fish Camp began last Saturday when all members plus Mard's future bride (Joelyn lasted 24 hours, a new Camp record for fiancés!) converged at the Hideaway Resort on the Turtle-Flambeau Flowage.

A night of revelry followed, the likes of which would not be seen again until the next night and the next until all The Boys had gone home again. There was music, laughter, pool, a couple pizzas I think, and Busch Light's good friend, Hamms the Beer Refreshing.

The next day dawned bright and early. About three hours later, all able anglers were on the lake. Two days later, LeGear went fishing, too. In a stunning display of angling finesse, we have collectively landed a mess of undersize northern pike and an out-of-season smallmouth bass.

The biggest news this week is that four tadpoles succumbed to an early demise in an act that will live in infamy. In short, they got gulped, and it wasn't by the bass.

After probing a weed bed for signs of life late one afternoon, I was rowing back to shore when I saw JK and Sam on the beach. JK was tipping his head back, then leaning forward and apparently spitting, causing Sam to convulse with laughter. Spit, laugh, spit, laugh—what was up?

The Boys were up to no good, again, and were engaged in a live tadpole swallowing contest! JK finally succeeded in gulping his frog in progress. Instead of shunning him for the rest of the week like good girls would do, The Boys determined that to be a man, they had to swallow a tadpole, too.

Amid much hooting, hollering, jumping up and down (The Boys, not the tadpoles), and turning bright red in the face, four tadpoles met an untimely end that afternoon. HB was just glad the contest was held outdoors so she didn't have to clean up after.

Slick took the title for most attempts, with eight tries before his tadpole finally stayed down. I even have a photo of its tail waving out the corner of his mouth. If it appeared on a postcard, the U.S. Mail would refuse delivery.

Lest you think Fish Camp is totally devoid of culture, we thrive on local history. Al Capone's brother, Ralph, had lived in Mercer and managed a bar on the main drag. Al enjoyed Mercer, too, and during wintertime visits would arrive at the bar by a horse-drawn sleigh.

Our second night at Camp, we visited Little Bohemia. It's a resort near Mercer where John Dillinger narrowly escaped capture by the FBI during a shootout in the 1930s. You can still see the bullet holes in the log walls that are liberally decorated with original newspaper stories.

On our way home to our own Hideaway, I piloted JK's van down winding roads with The Boys quietly (for once) crooning along to LeGear's CD. All hopped up on two near beers, I added my lilting alto to "Poncho and Lefty," "King of the Road," and "Sunday Mornin' Comin' Down."

Of course, I can't write a comprehensive postcard from Fish Camp and not mention the food. Slick does most of the cooking, which consists of throwing meat on a flaming grill until the grates disappear along with low flying birds. Chips and hot sauce are official Camp vegetables.

The days pass in a happy blur of morning mists, afternoon trips to town, flaming grills, and fishing. The fog blanketing the Flowage at night is our signal to head over to the lodge for tale swapping, pool playing, and libation appreciation.

Having a great time! Wish you were here. Love, Nancy

2. HUNTING UP TROUBLE

The Original Fast Food

Whenever my folks come to visit, I like to play a little game with them called 'Hide the Venison.' They detest the stuff, so I am morally obligated to try and break down their defenses, and help them learn to love the original fast food.

"What's in this stew?"

"My burger seems awfully dry."

"Hey, kids, let's go out to eat! Our treat!"

Mom and Dad haven't been up for a whole year now, and I can't say I don't know why. But when they come again, I've got a whole stew, I mean *slew* of disguised venison dishes planned, as well as a list of restaurants we'd like to hit.

Ever since the first cave spouse complained, "Woolly mammoth again? But it's so stringy!", man has struggled with the dilemma of how to make wild game taste like corn-fed beef. It's impossible of course, because a deer isn't a cow. If it was, hunters would dress like Holsteins.

However, you can still turn a deer into a tasty meal. The first trick in venison's transformation is to treat the meat like something you actually plan to eat. It starts with a pull of the trigger.

When a hunter shoots a deer, nature sends a wondrous substance raging through his body called adrenaline. Adrenaline helps him throw off his coat in sub-zero weather, plunge his arms into the animal's innards, scrub up with snow, then drag the deer out of the woods, sometimes so quickly it barely touches the ground.

This phenomenon is commonly known as, "The bigger the buck, the faster you go."

Some hunters produce so much adrenaline, they bypass vital steps, like properly cleaning their deer or remembering to untie it from the roof of the car after their long drive home. If your deer isn't processed soon after your triumphant return, it's going to taste a lot like US-41, heavily salted.

So, your deer is cleaned, unloaded, and skinned, and your children are all armed with age-appropriate butcher knives. Do you consult a professional butcher chart outlining specific cuts of meat? Only if you're still wearing that Holstein suit!

Venison consists of four cuts: big roasts, little roasts, steaks, and dry hamburger. For instance, hindquarters make big roasts, and necks make little ones. Backbones make steaks, and tenderloins are tenderloins. Everything else goes into the hamburger pot for this year's chili, spaghetti sauce, and other dishes my folks will only eat once.

Many hunters enjoy making venison sausage, which is a wonderful preparation for wild game. To make it, you cut your deer into bite-size chunks, then bag and place it in the freezer. Call the butcher shop to have your name put on a waiting list. Then live a long and happy life.

Just kidding! Butcher shops in the U.P. are very busy during deer season, but they eventually get to your order. Soon after, with a lot of help from assorted spices and a token barnyard animal for suet's sake, your deer is transformed into a socially acceptable lunch meat, like baloney.

Another popular treatment for venison is jerky. Jerky is a tasty option that can be made at home. It transforms fresh meat into edible leather, which will keep the hunter and his family busy chewing until they're finally called to come pick up their box of venison baloney.

Of course, there is always that Hunter's Helper called cream of mushroom soup. A rather drab substance on its own, it has long been recognized as *the* vehicle for wild game preparation. Groups opposed to hunting could probably bring the sport to a skidding stop, just by buying out all the cream of mushroom soup at local grocery stores.

But you didn't read that here.

The last tip I'm prepared to offer, besides never serving tallowy deer ribs with a cold drink, is to just can it. The process involves filling jars with bite-size pieces of venison, placing them in a pressure canner, and then cooking them until every fiber of that tough old buck's being hollers, "Uncle!"

Take a jar down off the shelf on those busy week nights, sneak it over to the stove so your folks and kids can't see it, and a few minutes later you too will be saying those words Americans everywhere so love to hear:

"Come and get your fast food!"

Boars, the Other White Meat

Ever since this little piggy went AWOL, inhabitants and guests of Upper Michigan's Point Abbaye have been fighting in vain to get the wild Russian boars returned to sender.

The clever Russkies staged a successful escape from their game farm, and have been wreaking havoc on local sensibilities since. The DNR was contacted right away, but patiently explained to the citizenry that, based on name alone, the wild Russian boar is obviously not a natural resource and is therefore out of its jurisdiction.

The state's stand is that the wild Russian boars are too far from Lansing to pose a serious threat to Michigan as legislators know it. However, if a bill addressing the problem in any way should materialize, we taxpayers should vote for whoever wrote/supports/can quote from it.

On the home front, local police could shoot, but have no experience whatsoever in the construction of wild boar blinds. Our area sportsmen's club could whip up a lovely booyah, but having already taken the "Let 'em go, let 'em grow," and when the spike returned that evening, I gratefully pulled the trigger.

As the Other White Meat Industry made clear not so long ago, our problem is all in the packaging. In the best American traditions of Turn That Frown Upside Down and my personal favorite, Have A Nice Day, we need to look at the bright side of harboring wild and possibly vicious boars by promoting the curly tails off of those big ol' golden pigs.

A few years back in Crystal Falls, it was discovered the town's forefathers had basically built on a big old hunk of fungus. In a stroke of pure genius, the townspeople put on their mushroom caps and came up with the Humongous Fungus Fest, a wildly profitable celebration of something most people wouldn't even eat, much less live on.

Our very own DNR proved it's a marketing giant with the reintroduction of moose into the U.P. Once native to the region, moose were dramatically brought back in the 1980s via a flurry of helicopters and schoolchildren bearing permission notes for a field trip to the moose landing site in Michigamme.

As we well know, the moose is not one of Mother Nature's better efforts. It has long, skinny legs, a hump on its back, and a nose that defies polite description. But thanks to a certain cartoon character named Bullwinkle and a brisk souvenir trade in all things moose-related, we have embraced the beast as one of our own.

Even though boars are large, vicious brutes with bad personal hygiene, there is no reason a similar marketing plan could not be built around their unfortunate residence in our county. Following the DNR's sage lead, it would have to start with the children.

The L'Anse Wild Russian Boars would certainly command more respect in athletic endeavors than mere L'Anse Hornets. If the team did begin to lag on the court or field, the coach could either liven up the action or end the suffering by loosening the bolt on the team mascot's cage.

Every small town has its signature celebrations, and a Wild Russian Boar Roast is a party just waiting to happen. Pig roasts have already proven popular at area taverns, graduation parties, and certain Point Abbaye residences. Why not let the pig out of the Point, and share the spread for the sake of the community?

Greased pig contests have long been a staple of county fairs, pitting squealing piglets against children and adults eager to pin the porker and win a prize. In this age of extreme sports, a greased Wild Russian Boar Contest is just the thing to keep both the economy and local hospital in good stead.

Of course, there will be those who sympathize with the wild Russian boars who were ripped from their homeland and have since gone astray. That's where the Wild Russian Boar Adoption Corner comes into play. Photos would be run on a weekly basis, and for just a few rubles, the public could "adopt" a boar running wild at Point Abbaye.

They wouldn't actually take a boar in. That's just plain dangerous. Instead, adoptive families would receive a blurry photo of their pig and a certificate bearing its name and estimated location. It would be like owning a star, only uglier.

At the end of a long season of boar roasts, greased boar contests and victories by the L'Anse Wild Russian Boars, the community would wrap up the fun with the highlight of the tourist season: The Running of the Boars.

We borrow this idea from Spain, where wild bulls once freely roamed the streets due to similar questions of jurisdiction. Finally, in a fit of rage, the people leaped in front of the bulls and led them out of the town, which then became overrun with CNN cameramen and assorted paparazzi.

Since the boars already run free, we would have to round up a few for this special event. And as long as we're going that far, we could box them up and fly them down to Lansing, where both the streets and laws are much more clearly defined.

Won't it be fun to finally see our legislators in action? See you at the capital! And don't forget to bring your permission note.

Home Sweet Deer Camp

My husband shut off his Sawzall and stepped back from the deer carcass slung over our kitchen table. Uncle Phil, seated across from him and in the direct line of fire, casually dipped a bone chip out of his coffee mug. Our other hunting guest, David, gingerly wiped deer hair off his glasses.

How had we come to this?

I'll tell ya' how. I went to the store one day before the firearm deer season opened and bought myself trouble in the form of a hunting license. If there's one thing I've learned over 20-some hunts, every one has its lessons. Another thing I've learned is, I will never learn.

Oh sure, we've picked up on some valuable pointers along the way. We spread hay on the floors of our blinds each year to insulate and muffle sound. It also covers some of the scent you haul in after wearing the same long handles two weeks running.

We've also learned the easiest way to skin a deer is with an ATV. Hang the deer, cut along the usual seams, then tie some Binder Twine around its scruff and shift into low gear. Be sure to use this year's twine so the driver isn't rear-ended by a flying buck.

Remember to dust off your scope (hunt of '93). Get good directions to your deer blind (hunt of '95), and if you gut shoot your deer (hunts of both '88 and '90), clean it out really well before your father-in-law sees it. You'll still catch h---, but it won't sting as badly.

The hunt of '07 was shaping up to be one for the books. A veritable parade of big bucks trekked across our fields in late summer and early fall. One day I watched a fork horn following a six-point that was trailing an eight-point buck. This would be the best hunting season ever!

On the opening day of firearm season, my husband told me I didn't have to shoot the first spike, or two-point buck, I saw. It went against my personal motto of "Let 'em go—to my blind!", but I foolishly nodded my hunting cap, and headed out.

Five does greeted me at dawn, and soon after, I spotted a spike moving in. I need glasses to read, but can spot a spike at a dead run through thick brush from roughly one county away. My eye doctor just needs more dynamic charts.

I raised my gun and watched him walk to the bait pile. He ate, visited with the gals, digested, flaunted my favorite broadside target from both sides, and then ambled back to where he came from. I held him in my sights right up until he disappeared.

Well! What a sportsman I was! And a little bit cold. And kind of hungry, and thoroughly disgusted with myself because it's never been about the horns. Why was I sitting out in the freezing woods with a gun across my lap if I wasn't allowing myself to shoot?

I "Let 'em go, let 'em grow" all afternoon, and when the spike returned that evening, I gratefully pulled the trigger. Across our 40 acres, my husband grinned in his blind, pretty sure we'd be enjoying wild veal again in the near future.

I haven't let a spike go since. I always dust my scope before I go out. I field dress my deer clean as a whistle. And after this year, I will never, ever allow a reciprocating saw in my house when the table is set with a dead deer.

I am not ordinarily one to pass the buck, obviously, but I'd have to say it's all Rob Aho's fault. The DNR wildlife biologist at the Baraga office taught me the neat trick of using a reciprocating saw to remove a deer's horns. The problem was, he never told me not to crank one up in the house.

Because the buck was size petite, meaning it was probably mine, we had brought the carcass indoors to remove the backbone steaks. We usually discard the ribs, but I wanted to try roasting a few this year, so my husband said he'd go back to the garage for his handsaw.

"Why not the reciprocating saw?" I happily suggested. "Works great!"

It wasn't all that dramatic. We live in a log home after all, and our hardwood floors clean up pretty easily. I think they shine even better now thanks to all that tallow. But I've seen enough talk shows to know when an intervention is in order, and I'm ready for company.

"Martha Stewart! Welcome to our humble home! How about some coffee? And let's accent that cup with a nice, tight lid."

Paint Ball Hunt

The U.P. firearm deer season has finally arrived, and you know what that means.

It's open season on hunters.

• Each year, various Associations for the Prevention of Cruelty to Animals that Were Not Raised in Barnyards (APCAWNRB for short) take aim at hunters. Their beef is that unarmed animals are being slaughtered in our scenic setting, even though the hunters promise to eat them afterwards.

It is hard to defend yourself in the face of such adversity, especially when (A) you have a firearm in one hand and a carrot in the other, and (B) the animals are so much cuter than the hunters, especially after the second week of deer camp.

It's an unfair battle right from the start, which is why I am proposing a win-win solution for both predators and prey alike: the Paint Ball Buck Hunt.

Unlike real live firearms, paint ball guns are socially acceptable. You're not actually maiming or killing your similarly armed friends. You're just going through the motions, while leaving sufficient evidence behind to prove, "I could have splattered you like the proverbial egg."

The Paint Ball Buck Hunt would follow the same time line as the regular firearm season. You would still have to purchase a license, even if you are a youth, to help support future paint ball deer management. Then you'd gun it for the nearest paint store to buy some ammunition.

The Paint Ball Buck Hunt action would start to heat up as hunters locked horns over preferred paint colors. Things could get messy and spills would be a given as the sportsmen competed for eye-fetching, buck-staining shades of paint.

"Hey, can ya' tell me if Misty Melon Madness is still available?"

"Back off, bud. He's mixin' up my Midnight in Paris!"

"Ha! Ya' call that a color? I'll bet your last buck was Peaches & Cream!"

The DNR Hunting Guide would figuratively go out the window, since safety in the woods would amount to not spilling paint. Instead, a Rules of Etiquette Guide would encourage respecting fellow hunters' territories, rights, and color choices, even if they are pastels.

Newspapers would do their part by adjusting Buck Lists to give both hunters and hues their due: *John Smith, six point buck, Nov. 15, Zesty Lemon Surprise*. It would be a win-win, as nothing makes newspapers fly off the racks faster than front page shots of big bucks in Technicolor.

The Paint Ball Buck Hunt would result in greater hunter success rates because there would be no limit on how many times a deer could be painted. As an added bonus, it would be even easier for hunters to hear big bucks coming in, because they'd kind of crackle when they walked.

As with any fresh and innovative idea, there are still a few glitches to work out. For instance, what would hunters have to eat after a long, successful Paint Ball Buck Hunt? And what would they hang on their walls after their trophies ran, dripping water-based latex, back into the swamp?

Finally, how would they determine the winners of all those Big Buck contests?

Well, most hunters could easily survive on all the leftover produce they brought to bait the deer, supplemented with socially acceptable pre-killed meats purchased at local stores. The woods are alive with game cameras during deer season, so buck shots could replace head mounts. You can't hang your coat on them, but they're easier to sneak onto the living room wall.

Painters, I mean "hunters," could submit big buck shots for prizes. In case of two-tone deer, the dominant hue would rule. Winners would take a bow, deer would take a bath, and a huge new corporate sponsor would be hailed as the true hero of the hunt: Sherwin Williams.

3. UP SCALE FASHION

"Toque" Spells Trouble

I have been accused of writing down to people.

Do you think that is true?

I do not. Not, not, not.

The stone was cast by a concerned friend (he works in the L'Anse Public Library—as the librarian) following a newspaper article that I wrote during the past deer season, in which I used the popular local term for winter hat: chook.

And that is exactly how I spelled it. Chook, chook, chook.

If you enjoy doing crossword puzzles or looking up obscure words in the dictionary so you can beat your friends at Scrabble, you know the proper spelling for chook is toque. I knew this, because a Q is worth 10 points in Scrabble, and I am one mean Scrabble player.

However, whenever I lay a toque on the board, my opponent invariably pounces.

"What are you trying to pull now? Gimme that dictionary!"

My reputation is cleared, my Q is used, and I can probably slip by with an actual misspelling later in the game.

Believe it or not, when I was a journalism student (that part is certifiable; it's what comes next that you might question), we were instructed to write at the *seventh-grade level*. Keep your paragraphs and your sentences short. Don't use words the reader might not understand. If your reader has to think, you're going to lose him.

Now, apart from having recently used the local term for winter hat, misspelled though it might have been, I am not in the habit of writing down to people. Sure, I did it for my professors, but that was only for a grade. I was one mean journalism student, too.

My personal belief is that each time you're exposed to a new word, you gain a better understanding of its meaning. Pay attention to the way it's used, and your vocabulary is bound to grow. If you like the word well enough, you may even use it yourself someday.

It might fit you like a chook.

For instance, I used a handful of words that were fairly new to me in an article I wrote last week. Some of them were even used in the proper context. They were, in order of appearance, *espoused*, *ombre*, *icon*, and *taboo schmaboo*.

Are these the words of a down-writer? When was the last time your seventh grader told you, "Mom, I can no longer espouse you as an icon because you drive an ombre minivan. Taboo schmaboo."

I would like to add that "schmaboo" is not a proper word, unless it is a word in some foreign language, and then it might not be a proper one. If that is the case, you didn't hear it from me.

So, if I am writing down to people, then how can I write up to them without making them slam my stories down on the floor and holler, "This is work! Where's my old seventh-grade reader?"

Well, I use colloquialisms, like "chook" and "popple" and "I caught a snake (small pike) at Worm Lake," but then I throw in some responsible vocabulary to balance it all out, like "colloquialisms." I write to kindergarteners and to quantum physicists, sometimes all in the same sentence.

I don't remember how to write on the seventh-grade level, and I didn't save any of my old textbooks to help refresh my memory. But I do remember how we learned our vocabulary words way back in the seventh grade.

Our teacher was Mr. Silhan, an inspired educator who inspired respect and fear in us by having the physique of Mt. Everest. Rumor had it he used to wrestle professionally, and that was enough to make me behave, because who wants to be thrown out of class after first being spun three times over your teacher's head?

Mr. Silhan taught vocabulary by allowing a student to pick a word out of the dictionary each day, post it on the bulletin board, and then share its definition with the class. That unrelated, oddball, but totally relevant list was then included in our weekly spelling test.

I can still see Ed Kenny standing "akimbo," and remember my own personal search for just the right word. And who among us will ever forget the day Bill Gleason tacked his selection up, walked boldly to the front of the deathly silent classroom, and exclaimed, "It is a female dog."

Bill became a seventh-grade icon, and is probably writing for some wildly popular media today. But that is not the way I care to write. I much prefer to follow the example of two former co-workers, who never spoke down to one another unless they'd consulted a dictionary first.

They were my best friend, Cheri, and my brother, Mark, at Pizza Castle on Chicago's South Side. She worked inside making pizzas, he delivered, and whenever they were scheduled to work together, the sophisticated insults would fly.

"How ya' doing, you insouciant reprobate?"

"Why, I'm fine, you obtuse gormandizer. And yourself?"

They'd ask each other how to spell the big words, taking careful notes. After work and back home again, they checked their dictionaries to learn how badly they'd been maligned, then gleefully prepared for their next verbal attack.

And just where did all that vocabulary work get them?

Mark is a retired Army major, and Cheri is a Consultant for Senior Living Dining Services and Campus Development. And me? I'm a highly acclaimed Northwoods journalist! Just ask the L'Anse librarian.

School Clothes Naturally Cool

I walked into the store with my daughter and granddaughter and stopped dead, and it wasn't because I'd forgotten what I needed. I had stumbled onto the scene of a horrific crime.

Someone had taken all the jeans off their racks, scattered them on the floor, and driven over them with a brush hog. Then they'd neatly hung the remains back on the racks just in time for back to school sales.

There were gaping holes in the knees. Other areas were worn threadbare before they'd even been worn. Some pant legs had been shortened but not hemmed, their uneven strings left dangling down like so many casualties from Shark Week.

As my little granddaughter came skipping up behind me, I moved to block her view from the carnage. I was one skip too late. Her smile beamed right through the clothing remains as she excitedly assessed the damage.

"Those are SOOOOO COOL!"

Sensing a teaching moment, I looked down at our little shopper and said, "They're all torn up." Sensing a shopping moment, she

Looking cool for the start of the new school year comes naturally thanks to current fashion. The model kept her cool, too, until the photographer offered to run for her sewing kit. Then the shoot ended.

shrugged and replied, "They're pretty," and went back to admiring the rags on the racks.

The distressed look has been in fashion ever since people quit honestly earning it. Consumers used to buy new clothes and engage in hard labor that reduced them to tatters. Consumers now buy tattered clothes and work from their homes so they can pay more for less.

You do not have to be a baby boomer (can barely compute, but has common sense to spare) to appreciate the fact clothes ought to be fully intact when you buy them. People pay good money for their personal apparel. They have the right to expect the clothing industry to tie off its knots.

Back when the Brady Bunch still roamed the earth and Flipper vied with Lassie for Most Bumbling Human Saves Per Week, I obviously watched way too much TV. Also, the only back to school fashion choice moms had to make was whether their boys were Rustlers or Wranglers.

Both brands were 100 percent cotton and wore like iron. Boys marched off to their first day of school like The Nutcracker because their knees couldn't bend. When full mobility was finally restored, the tiniest air leak was immediately snuffed by Mom's sewing kit.

Rips were mended. Holes were patched. Pants were bought big to last the school year, then rolled up because hemming was just a waste of good material. Some kids' blue jean cuffs were so big they walked to school bowlegged.

This is not the fashion in which parents now raise their children. Modern kids have Spandex in what's left of their jeans! They could wear them to dance in The Nutcracker, if it weren't for all those strings left dangling by the brush hog.

Stay safe this new school year, kids. Your new jeans already guarantee you're cool.

Bagging Mrs. U.P. Title

"You can be Mrs. U.P.!"
Please disregard this invitation by coordinators of the upcoming pageant. You can't be Mrs. U.P., because I'm gonna'.

Even though I am a naturalized U.P. citizen, I feel I have racked up an impressive list of Mrs. U.P. qualifications. First of all, I married a U.P. mister. Then, even though the duration of winter and bloodsucking insect seasons is unbelievably long up here, we did not cross the bridge and escape to lower Michigan.

Of course, it takes a lot more than a wedding ring and alternating cases of frostbite and anemia to earn the Mrs. U.P. title. According to the rules, "the pageant strives to recognize today's married woman's role as a wife, mother, professional and civic or charitable volunteer, as well as her other accomplishments."

Working mom. Civic stuff. Charity case. I believe the pageant has just described Nancy!

If you, too, fit the label, the competition is straightforward enough. In fact, it is a bit too straightforward. The run for the title of Mrs. U.P. consists of just three categories: an interview, aerobic wear, and evening gown judging. The organizers even had the gall to add, "there are no talent or swimsuit competitions."

Well I can tell you, it was a bitter blow to learn that I will not be allowed to field dress and pressure can a whitetail deer for the Mrs. U.P. talent competition. The new swimsuit I bought at Fleet Farm just three short years ago would have wowed the judges, too, as long as they could see past my "farmer tan" to truly appreciate it.

Worst of all, where am I supposed to get some "aerobic wear?"

I don't know what civic situation those judges were born into, but I can assure you that aerobic wear doesn't see a lot of daylight in the U.P. Sure, some women wear it, and a select few even fit in it, but most of us prefer to exercise in comfier packaging.

If we absolutely have to do something aerobic, we wear our threadbare yoga pants (threadbare on the seat only), our husbands' ripped t-shirts and our gardening sneakers, preferably the ones with Velcro closures. And we never, EVER wear aerobic wear in public.

The evening gown competition is just as unlikely. The only formals U.P. women wear are ones we bought for our high school proms and for standing up in friends' weddings, specifically designed to make the brides look better.

In both cases, by the time a U.P. woman attains both the title and trappings of "Mrs.", neither is likely to fit.

Personally speaking, I'd prefer a competition with more regional flair. How about a contest to see how much firewood you can stack in your pickup before the driver following you has to shift into "slalom" gear? Or how many loads of wash you can hang on your line before it hits the dirt?

Rules are rules, but that doesn't mean they can't be slightly bent. For my interview, I plan to sprinkle my responses with lots of local color, and flaunt my worldliness with a few Finnish phrases—carefully avoiding ones I've both heard and used while picking my laundry up off the ground.

The most aerobic thing I do is snowshoe, and I anticipate cutting quite a swath through the competition thanks to footwear alone. Teamed with my down jacket that leaks feathers and my snow pants that still bear evidence of a good ice fishing season, I'm sure to have the judges swooning in my wake.

For my grand finale, I am planning an evening gown that will absolutely dazzle what is left of the crowd. Borrowing heavily from a dress made of gold credit cards that I saw several years ago during the Oscars telecast, I'm saving up my canning lids for a U.P. twist on a red carpet winner.

I can see my family now, hoisting (I mean, "helping") me onstage as I fairly glitter with Ball and Kerr canning jar lids, still bearing labels marked "Chokecherry jelly," "Pickled beets" and "Fleet beef, 1996," as the song I've so longed to hear blares in the background:

"Theeeere she is! Missus Yoo-ooper!"

Boot Bench Runs Deep

These boots are made for walking, and mucking, and mudding, and hunting, and—

You catch my drift. If Nancy Sinatra had styled her 1966 break-out hit, "These Boots are Made For Walking" after life in the U.P. she'd have enjoyed a professional career of relative obscurity.

Unless she crossed the bridge, and then she'd be a sellout everywhere from prayer breakfasts to VFW fish frys.

That's right, I mean the Mighty Mackinac Bridge, gateway to a region where a woman can't survive without a stack of footwear to select from. "Snow" does not begin to describe the range of boots a woman needs to navigate in the U.P.

The truth was brought to light by my friend, Elaine Dougovito, who recently found herself defending her collection. She and a friend from Georgia, which is one of your sandals states, were discussing footwear, and Elaine owed up to owning about 10 pairs of boots.

The woman was appalled. Why would anyone need 10 pair of boots? Was Elaine the Imelda Marcos of the Northwoods?

Tut tut I say, in direct reference to the Egyptian ruler who also sported sandal tan lines. In a land where crop pants or capris qualify as shorts, Elaine might actually be lagging a bit in her high-rising footwear collection.

Northwoods women have good reason for deep boot benches. We require substantial coverage for all four seasons of the year. Each presents different challenges to our collection. Hardly any of them have anything to do with fashion.

Take spring. I mean it. You can have it. We start out with felt-lined winter boots. Then we downgrade to insulated mud boots. When it really heats up, we break out our rain boots. Then it's date night—dare we dazzle him with our new hiking boots?

Don't be a fool! We'll need those for both weeks of summer.

Sandals would also suffice for those precious few warm days, but we'd need to accessorize with bracelets declaring our blood types. Mosquitoes love a sandaled presentation. Just check their tiny postings on Facebook.

The kids are barely back to school when we step out onto the deck one morning and our feet forget to stop. Then the rest of us hits the deck, because thanks to the early arrival of ol' Jack Frost, "fall" refers to more than just leaves in the U.P.

After dusting ourselves off, we start doing the boot shuffle in reverse, adding layers of insulation as each pair leaves us cold. Then it's ice fishing season and we break out the big guns: our brother's inflatable Army boots, because it is far better to float upside down than not at all.

Wait. That might just be me. But I am still in good company when it comes to boot collections, which also include your go to town boots, your go to a bigger town boots, cross country ski boots, boot slippers and, tucked away in a dark corner, those shiny new flip-flops with the plastic daisy on top.

Because a U.P. girl can always dream.

Clearly High Fashion

There's a new trend in the fashion world this spring. It is called "Clothes You Can See Through."

No it's not, because nobody ever got to be a rich fashion designer by telling the god's truth. It is called "layering," because you have to pile on about three layers to adequately conceal what the good Lord gave you.

The trend became transparent to me when I was looking for a new top to wear for Easter. I was looking through the rack straight through to the hardware in the middle because the fabric wasn't stout enough to stop me.

The tops were there alright—I could see their price tags just fine—but they were filmy and sheer and lacking in substance. When I tried to take one off the rack, the tops on either side slipped their hangers and fluttered to the floor.

If it wasn't for their floral print, they'd have disappeared altogether.

There has always been a place in the fashion world for clothes that lack substance. It is called the Lingerie Department. Anything slightly risqué winds up there, and men walk wide circles around it on their way to Sporting Goods.

Now lingerie can occur anywhere because sheer has gone mainstream. The men have nowhere to run, and the women can't hide either because you can see right through our clothes.

Sheer is here to stay, but people in my baby booming age group still struggle to accept it. That is because we were raised to buy clothes by the pound. Our mothers bought our clothes a size too big which we wore until they were a size too small, then passed down to the next sibling in line.

Our papas didn't win The Big One so our mamas could buy clothes you could see through. Cotton, canvas, and khaki served our country well and were good enough for its kids. Our blue jeans were even double-riveted, quite possibly by Rosie the Riveter.

It took some wear before our clothes could actually bend. If the wind wasn't whipping when our moms hung the wash, we were back to walking stiff as soldiers. Our clothes were a bit scratchy, too, but we all scratched together as a country.

Now we are just scratching for some coverage. And we can get it, too, if we are just willing to keep adding layers until the sun quits shining through our clothes.

I finally despaired of finding something suitable for breaking bread and hard-boiled eggs with the rest of the congregation on Easter morning. So I decided on Plan B, which is usually Plan A anyway, and headed for the St. Vincent DePaul thrift shop.

The woman who wore my gently used top before me was a neat eater, or a wonder at getting out stains. The top was short sleeved, kind of silky, yet substantial enough that it didn't let the light shine through.

Though I am sure my inner light added a little glow, because I got it for just six bits.

4. KEEP ON TRUCKIN'

UP in the Air

Q: Is it safe to fly?

A: No.

Q: How about now?

A: Still not feelin' it.

The fabricated dialogue above illustrates a harsh truth: I am not afraid to make up stuff to illustrate my point. And my point is that it is never entirely safe to fly into, out of, or miles above the U.P.

The problem with the U.P. is, nothing. I might be a fabricator, but I'm no fool. I love my homeland! The airline industry is the clear villain in this tale of missed connections, destinations and luggage, set in the peninsula that enjoyed a cameo in "The Wreck of the Edmund Fitzgerald."

Ever since Wilbur turned to Orville and asked, "How could you forget the peanuts?", man has struggled to make his peace with air travel. The Wrights' chief concern was getting off the ground. Nowadays, it's all about sealing the deal.

Shortly after the Wrights landed, travel agents populated the earth, and it was good because everyone was on the same page. You purchased your airline ticket from a travel agent who neatly sealed it in an envelope and sent it to your home via the good ol' U.S. mail.

A short century later, you purchase your ticket with the help of a child/grandchild who knows how to navigate the internet. After carefully selecting the proper airport, destination, and seat, you save your information because your printer is out of ink.

The next step in the process, after going to town for more ink, is worrying yourself sick because you live in the U.P. and have just purchased an expensive, non-refundable airline ticket. You worry about snow, fog, wind, and all those deer between home and the airport that are waiting to board your car grill.

If you arrive safely and on time and your flight is on schedule, slap yourself hard because you're most likely dreaming. Then slap yourself again, because you overpaid for your flight.

Thanks to travel miles, credit card rewards, and coupons, every other passenger on your flight is guaranteed to have paid less air fare than you. Your only guarantee is a seat in the airport terminal next to the chatty passenger who paid the least.

Once you have awakened to reality—your flight is delayed in Green Bay, WI, out of habit—you settle into your plastic molded chair to read airline magazine stories about all the beautiful locations your airline currently isn't flying into.

Time goes by. Child passengers grow up and go out into the world on shuttle buses. College students earn their degrees online, then work remotely from the airport terminal. You start getting your vending machine coffee at the senior rate.

Then one magical day, your boat comes in: it's your flight! The snow is gone, the wind has died, the fog is temporarily lifted, and there are currently no deer on the runway. You hobble onboard, drop into your seat, and notice too late there's something awfully familiar about the passenger beside you.

It's Gordon Lightfoot, pen in hand, all set to write his next big hit.

Driving Me Crazy

People often turn to reporters in time of need.

--They need you to cover a big event.

--They need you to promote an important cause.

--They need you to lend them your pen so they can sign their kid off the team bus.

Sometimes people turn to you because they have been wronged and are seeking justice. They will have to buy your newspaper to read all about it, but it is still cheaper than an attorney and they get the bowling scores besides.

Well, I need someone to step up for me. I'd do it myself, but that would compromise my objectivity. Also, some mom made off with my pen after the girls' JV volleyball game last week.

I have been wronged. Anyone interested in a big exposé on the car tire industry?

As I wait for a reporter to come to my aid, allow me to state my case. I drive down lots of rough and rutted roads. They are called Michigan major highways. I also drive on gravel roads, woods roads, and the occasional paved stretch. They are your Michigan streets and side roads.

All that driving tends to wear my tires thin, so this past May I bought four brand new tires rated to last for 60,000 miles. In a perfect and not terribly scenic world, they should have gone the distance. I got as far as September.

One flat is not going to help me bring down the tire industry. However, the two flats I got over two days last week should get me, at the very least, a cut on my next road hazard package. Depends on the reporter covering my case.

I was driving down a side road in Covington on Tuesday when I suddenly heard a loud hissing noise from the back of my car. With snake season officially over, it could mean only one thing. I needed a cell phone, pronto!

Cell phone service is spotty in the U.P., so loving and concerned husbands always make sure their wives are equipped with a sturdy car jack before they leave home. They'd equip us with a hanky to wave for help, but during firearm deer season it would just draw fire.

It's hard to play the damsel in distress card when you've reported about Fish Camp, my annual worship at that Northwoods altar of excess. I'm not a damsel in distress. I am clearly one distressing damsel. So I got out and changed my flat.

At the tire shop that night, I learned the puncture was too close to the sidewall to be repaired. I got $50 credit on an $80 tire, bought a bag of candy to celebrate excellent car jack service in Covington, and headed home.

The very next day I pulled into the grocery store parking lot and heard the snake again. This time, a large rock was poking out the center of my quickly deflating tire, which could mean only one thing: I should have bought a bigger bag of candy.

I threw open my trunk with a string of Fish Camp-worthy oaths, and grabbed the spare tire and tools. Then I jacked up the car while the tire gasped its last into my ear. I wasn't impressed. I'd heard that line just yesterday.

At the tire shop that night, I learned this puncture was so big you could throw a cat through it. I got $80 credit for my $80 tire, bought another bag of candy to help shorten my miserable life, and drove back home.

I brought the flat tire home because most of it was still brand new, and my husband is a whiz with a patch kit. When he looked at it, he laughed aloud, kind of maniacally I thought, because my car had apparently been attacked by a Great White Shark.

The gleaming piece of quartz embedded in my tire was shaped just like a tooth. He pulled it before I could snap a photo, which is unfortunate in light of my future legal case, but I would be happy to repeat his maniacal laugh for the sake of the jury.

It has been a full five days now since I have experienced my last flat tire. I'm getting so confident, I'm almost ready to roll my car out of the garage again, but I'm still waiting to hear from the reporter on my case.

I just hope she remembered to pack her car jack before she left home.

Dirty Cars Save Lives

Drivers across America owe a debt of gratitude to Jeremy Taylor.

Taylor and his dog were stranded in his vehicle for five days in the forest, and survived on packets of taco sauce. That means in the land of the free and home of the take-out, we Americans are not just slobs on wheels. We are canny survivalists!

It all started when Taylor, 36, and Ally, something in dog years, went for a ride in his Toyota 4Runner. While driving on a forest service road, they got stuck in deep snow.

So Taylor went to sleep. When he woke up the next day, his vehicle was still stuck, so he opted to walk out. Then his feet got stuck, so he returned to the vehicle to wait for help. Meanwhile, it kept on snowing.

If you have ever been stuck in deep snow with no relief in sight, you know that the first thing you should do is turn to your husband/boyfriend and bellow, "I told you not to go down this road!" The second thing you should do is check the back seat for supplies.

Everyone should have a survival kit in their vehicle. It should include a warm blanket, flashlight, energy bars so healthful you would only eat them to survive, and matches to cook the wild animals you catch in your snares.

Oh, and snares.

Nobody does this. Our glove boxes are stuffed instead with broken tire-pressure gauges, expired vehicle registrations, and receipts from the auto parts store. In case of emergency, our survival plan is a swan dive into the backseat.

The backseat is the official depository for all things we cannot bear to part with, but can't bother to bring into the house. They include mittens without partners, grimy baseball hats, and takeout condiments that are never actually eaten.

Like crackers. And taco sauce. Also, ketchup, mayo, sugar, powdered creamer, jam, jelly, salt & pepper, and, if you order extra greasy, hand wipes.

If you travel with children, you could conceivably sit out the season in a snowbank and still have leftovers to share with your rescuers. Children cannot travel without eating, and they cannot eat without dropping food. It is the real reason their car seats come with expiration dates.

Being of the bachelor persuasion, Taylor's survival menu lacked some of your major backseat food groups, like Goldfish and Cheez-Its. But his taco sauce packets proved a real lifesaver because they are technically a vegetable.

He was stuck in the snowbank for three days before someone finally noticed his chair was empty, and a missing man and dog alert immediately went out. Two short days later, a snowmobile rider bumped into them in the woods, and they were rescued.

In true pioneer spirit, Taylor and Ally were transported to the intersection of two forest service roads where they were reunited with family and friends. Hopefully his rescuers stopped for takeout along the way, preferably tacos to go with his leftover sauce.

The Biker Wave

I am a proud member of the brotherhood of bikers.

I know what you are thinking: "But you drive a sensible Corolla!" This is true, but only because my daughters won't let me bungee cord the grandchildren's car seats to the bike, even though it would eliminate back seat squabbles because you can't hear the kids over the wind.

But I can still be a biker, even if I'm just a hanger-on. When my husband rolls his dusty '83 Honda Gold Wing out of the garage, I am a woman transfixed. Then I am a woman transformed. I drop the green beans, turn off the pressure canner, and rip off my apron to hit the open road.

That last sentence was two parts fiction, but only for the sake of emphasis and to further enhance my edgy biker image. Nobody turns off the canner before the beans are done, and I only wear an apron on Thanksgiving because the bird tends to fight back.

The rest is spot-on. I ride with my husband and a strong sense of faith, never roaring away from home without a short consult with God first, including a request for critter control because it's always deer season on Michigan roadways.

And as you can tell from all those bikers out there, I am not the only one tugging on God's ear. Michigan roadways are full of motorcycles, at least until the first snowflake falls, and then we're back inside our sensible Corollas breaking up fights in the back seat.

Until then we are a brotherhood, and it's got nothing to do with gangs or bar fights or clothing choices that lean heavily toward black Angus. No, it's all about the wave.

I didn't know about the wave until the third time I rode with my husband. The first two times I kept my eyes closed. The third time, I opened them to see a fellow motorcyclist riding past with his hand jutting out to the side, fingers extended, and palm facing downward.

"WHAT?" I thought in capital letters, holding on even tighter and regretting my decision to peek. "We're already plummeting along at death-defying speeds with no seat belts on, and he's letting go with one hand?"

After we'd gotten home and my husband had pried my arms from his sides, he explained that's just what bikers do. They wave to one another.

According to my laptop, which is a real whiz at both trivia and spellchecker, the biker wave dates back to 1904. Arthur Davidson and William Harley passed one another on their motorcycles and exchanged a happy wave, probably because they'd just dusted a Schwinn. A passer-by assumed it was biker etiquette, and the wave was born.

Ever since that fateful day, bikers have been letting go to spread the love, and I'm right there with them. I wave at Harleys, Hondas, Yamahas, and just recently, a man pedaling a recumbent bicycle alongside the highway. He happily waved back.

The thing about the biker wave is, you have to do it right or your arm can fly off, just like your mom used to threaten when you stuck it out the car window as a kid. Biker joke! I warned you that I was edgy.

Seriously, if you raise your arm at 55 mph, your hand will just flap wildly in the wind. That is the reason for the official biker wave, which is both subtle and streamlined and prevents the brotherhood from slapping ourselves silly while greeting each other on the road.

Ride hard or stay home. And don't forget to wave.

License to Kill, and Spin

Q: What Michigan license allows you to harvest whitetail deer all year round?

A: Your driver's license!

It is an unsupported fact but highly likely that sooner or later, every Michigan driver will hit a whitetail deer. I have nicked two so far. My husband can meet that, and raise it by a moose. Haven't filled your Michigan driver's license yet? We've got you covered.

Deer, moose, and the occasional rogue cow can occur on Michigan roadways any time of year, but deer traffic is heaviest in the fall. Fall is the time of year when all a buck wants to do is find a date. All a doe wants to do is run away from a buck, preferably in front of your vehicle.

Michigan drivers don't really want to harvest their own meat with their cars, but it is hard to avoid a large ruminant bounding across the roadway between your headlights. You'd think the industry would take note and bring back hood ornaments, this time with cross hairs.

Instead I have seen vehicles, usually heavily dented, with a small warning whistle mounted on their hoods. When your whistle quits, you know you have a deer stuck in it.

Modern technology can outfit cars with GPS systems that tell you where to go and how to get there, and cameras that show you what you are backing into, but it cannot prevent you from filling your Michigan license this fall driving season.

Take some tips from someone with two notches on her steering wheel.

First, try and catch a ride with a friend. When that fails, select the shabbiest vehicle in your fleet and proceed with caution. If you spot deer loitering along the roadside, slow down. If you spot one in your lane, beep vigorously and prepare to meet your air bag.

If a deer accidentally manages to safely cross the road in front of your vehicle, you're not out of the woods yet. Deer often travel in pairs or small groups, carefully spaced for maximum impact. Watch for stragglers, which tend to run faster than the first wave.

If you don't hit them first, deer will sometimes take the initiative and ram your vehicle from the side. Then they retreat back into the woods where they won't be seen again until deer hunting season has ended, when they return for another round of car tagging. And this time, they've got a grudge.

The second major bump in Michigan roads, after the dead deer, is winter driving.

The season officially begins when you turn on the news to see some poor putz in the ditch. A wrecker is angling in to hook him up, and a grave-faced reporter in the foreground is warning, "Winter's here, and people have forgotten how to drive in the snow."

I do not think we forget how to drive. I think it is the U.P., and sooner or later, we're all the poor putz in the ditch.

There are some winter mornings where releasing your brake after turning your ignition key qualifies as driving too fast for conditions. Your wheels spin like that poor little girl's head in *The Exorcist*. And you use her bad language, too.

Unfortunately, most of us still have to continue on because only teachers were smart enough to get snow days written into their contracts. We spin our way down to bare ground and tentatively ease out onto the roadway, thanking our Maker that at least the deer are no longer dating.

Some people do drive too fast for conditions. They drive too fast all year round. In the winter, the special effects are even more spectacular because they raise a rooster tail of snow as they hit the ditch, sometimes right up to their door handles.

The rest of us hit the ditch, too, because sometimes you can do everything right and it still goes wrong. All four wheels hit ice at the same time, and all you can do is swear loudly and hang on for the ride, hoping a friend shows up before the law or a camera-wielding reporter.

The good news is, it's the U.P., and the volunteer response time for most ditch-outs is faster than a NASCAR tire crew. People tend to help each other out up here, because we know we're all in it together. I mean winter, not the ditch.

In case of emergency, I personally am useless, but will spin around as quickly as I can and offer a ride to a phone, unless the driver was smart enough to hit a ditch with cell service. Luckily, I've so far always been beaten to the scene by an angel of mercy, typically driving a heavily dented pickup truck.

Drive safely, try not to fill your Michigan driver's tag, and please stop for the putz in the ditch. Especially if it's me.

5. DOES NOT COMPUTE

Laptop Minding My Businesses

Dear *hp*,

I am writing to express my concern about the behavior of one of your laptop computers. It is minding my own business.

I know what you are thinking because I Googled it: "The purpose of the computer is to perform calculations, store information, retrieve data and process information. The computer will only do what it is programmed to do."

"Pshaw!" I say, because that is how I am programmed. Also because I never programmed my computer to store everything I ever typed in its little chip brain so it could turn my words against me in the form of disturbing pop-up ads.

The main problem, besides your sassy little *hp* laptop that is probably storing this complaint in its skewed memory for future pop-ups (*Got a complaint? Call Reiman & Frisk!*), is the delicate nature of my business.

I write columns for a weekly newspaper. My taste in subject matter is, how shall we say it? "Eclectic." Recent hot topics have included but are not limited to noodle ball, rare members of the chameleon family, and a robotic vacuum named Astro.

If you are me, it all makes perfect sense.

The problem is, you can't just sit down and write a thought-provoking column about robotic vacuums. First you've got to check out what your friends are doing on Facebook. Then you've got to play a game of free online solitaire. Then you have to reheat your coffee.

Finally, you need to research the various features of robotic vacuums. Typing the question is all it takes to open Pandora's Box or, even worse, enable your *hp* laptop to plague you for the rest of your writing days with senseless pop-ups.

The day after writing about Astro, I was checking out the news on my laptop when the first visual assault occurred. It was *Robotic Vacuums at Black Friday Prices!* Shortly after, I paid the price again with *Robo Vacs Under $300!*, and I'm still being taxed by the industry.

Same goes for chameleons. I'll be cruising the internet, nice as can be, when all of a sudden an ugly lizard will pop up on my screen to inform me of a new development in the ugly lizard news world, like the ugly chameleon finally found a date.

This was not the case back when I was packing my powder blue portable typewriter, the one with the missing E keypad. I swore every time I hit the sharp type bar, and it never pop-upped back at me with a *Get a new @#! key pad!*

A longer while back, I wrote a sensitive and thought-provoking piece on Barbie dolls. Imagine if you will my horror at the ensuing barrage of pop-up ads for Barbies, Kens, and their assorted and immense wardrobes which are actually much nicer than my own.

In conclusion, *hp*, I hope you will program your future laptops to mind their own beeswax and let this struggling reporter type her work in peace. Right after I've beaten my personal best online solitaire game time of 3:43.

Giving *hp* a piece of my mind, even though it already knows what I am thinking, right after I check to see who's doing what on Facebook.

Life's a Breach

People assume that as you grow older you get a bit paranoid, which leads me to inquire, "WHO'S ASKING? DO I KNOW THESE PEOPLE? AND ARE THEY ARMED?"

Of course, that's just plain ridiculous. I am not threatened by people with arms. I am threatened by people with keyboards who wreak havoc on our nation's computer network, which is perfectly secure except for when it is being breached.

I give you several of my accounts. Not literally, because I don't even recall which ones they were, but more than once in my increasingly paranoid past I've received warnings that one of my online accounts may have been breached.

The warning cards state that my personal private information—social security number, credit history, actual weight—may be in the hands of the criminal element. I need to act immediately to secure my information. And they want me to do it over the internet!

My heart skips a beat. Then it pounds a little harder to catch up. Then it settles right back down again and I tuck the card in with all my other warning cards, behind my Menard's rebates. Which, by the way, are printed on actual paper.

The world is getting away from paperwork. While trees everywhere raise their limbs to exchange high fives, for someone who works for a newspaper, this is not good news.

Schools are getting away from books, urging kids to plug into reading. Churches are moving from hymnals to wide screens. Newspapers sell online subscriptions, too, but thankfully, most Yoopers still prefer their news in wood stove-starting form.

Speaking as one who is too old for school, sleeps in on Sundays, and gets her newspapers for free because she works for one, I have no complaints. As one who still pays her bills with a checkbook, pull up a chair.

My husband and I prefer to pay our bills with checks because that's how we were raised. Our parents paid their bills with checks. So did our grandparents. Our great-grandparents sometimes paid with chickens, but it's much easier to slip a check into a mailbox than a chicken.

Businesses today don't even want our checks. They would prefer we give them our personal, private information so they can automatically withdraw our funds to cover our bills. This is where we get the term, "fox in the hen house."

While evil people armed with keyboards tap into yet another of my accounts, allow me to explain. I too was once a trusting consumer who allowed direct withdrawal for a subscription. It allowed our kids to order up to 10 terrible videos per month. Some months, they ordered the same terrible video twice.

The kids were grown and gone, and we were still receiving lists of terrible videos we'd already seen so we could place our monthly order. The web site wouldn't tell us how to end the agreement. There was no number to call. There was no address. We'd sold our souls for $10 a month.

We got them back somehow, but it took a lot of scrolling down and our strongest reading glasses. They're the same ones we now use to write checks to businesses with increasingly longer names, like United Health Care Insurance Co. Of America From Sea To Shining Sea.

I did stretch that one out a bit, but only to prove my point. There's a conspiracy afoot to wear down the last of us check writers. Some businesses don't even include envelopes anymore with our bills, and if they do, they add a reminder to "Save a stamp, use online payment!"

I'd rather mail them a chicken.

Net vs. Newspapers

When people tell me the internet is making newspapers obsolete, I unfriend them.

It's nothing personal. I just refuse to subscribe to their level of negativity because (A) I happen to work in print media, and (B) newspapers treat their readers better than any news source they can pull up on a screen.

I know this as a fact because I also put in my share of screen time. I start first thing in the morning, when I open my laptop to check my mail. Later on, I walk to the mailbox to check my other mail, which the internet is supposedly also making obsolete.

I'd unfriend the internet, too, but then I'd have to buy more stamps.

So I boot right up, and the first thing I see are the top stories of the day. The big news this morning, in order of appearance, was

"How to Crack an Egg Perfectly" and "She Scammed Dozens so She Could Stay at the Ritz."

Neither of these stories would ever make the front page of our hometown newspaper, unless the lady who scammed dozens was local. Even then, the only Ritz we've got in town are the crackers, which would have her lodging in the snack food aisle at the IGA.

Or Larry's Market. Gotta' stay objective.

The internet reports hard news, too, but in small servings with many sides of light features. For instance, there was also a "Mexican Border Wall Update," a "Government Gets Back to Work" piece, and a lengthy look at "What the Walton Family Looks Like Today."

Newspapers do not dumb down their news stories with light features, no matter how hard the years have been on Mary Ellen. They tell it like it is and run it right where it belongs, up front and in mostly black and white because color is too costly.

Like a nosy neighbor, the internet keeps careful tabs on every key that's tapped. It then uses its knowledge for evil, peppering my screen with annoying pop-up ads geared to my own personal private interests.

For example, when the U.P. is caught in the grip of yet another polar vortex, I like to browse hotel rates in Florida. The internet takes note, and the very next day a gray-haired (did I mention I'm also slightly mossy?) man pops up in the middle of my screen, offering to make me a reservation.

Thank you, but I am not that kind of gal.

Newspapers do not engage in this type of rude familiarity. When I open my newspaper, I see exactly what my neighbor is reading. That's why I turn to Classifieds first thing at the peak of rummage sale season, and Church News when it's Christmas Cookie Walk time at United Lutheran.

Newspapers don't share my information unless I've behaved badly and the neighbors need to be warned. Newspapers don't run uncomplimentary pictures of me, either, unless some wiseacre has purchased a Happy Ad for my birthday.

If they do, the ad sticks to its appointed page (thankfully, buried in Lifestyle) and doesn't pop up in unsuspecting readers' margins. Same goes for store inserts, those fliers tucked inside newspapers, unless they escape and then they just wind up on the floor.

At the end of the day, while others are still staring at their glowing screens, I and those I haven't unfriended can rest easy knowing we've already read all the news that's fit for print.

Reporter Drones On

I know I tend to drone on and on, but imagine how much worse it will be in the future when I am replaced by an actual drone?

The writing is on the wall. Actually, it's in *Editor & Publisher,* the monthly magazine that is all about the newspaper industry. As a newly minted college graduate 35 short years ago, I turned to *E&P's* Help Wanted section to score a job where I could both report and fish, not necessarily in that order.

Now a fairly wrinkled version of my former self, I turned to its pages again last week to learn that drones want to take it all away.

I saw it with my own eyes, right after I'd put on my reading glasses, under a section that did not even exist in *E&P* back in 1981: "All Things Digital." It said new regulations would soon allow local newspapers to use drones for reporting, taking photos and videos.

First of all, I would like to note that my readers are only 150X magnification. I need them for reading small print and finding bones while eating northern pike. Second, we don't even shoot videos at the newspaper. A drone, even if it was fresher-faced, would be overqualified for my job.

Drones are all over the news these days as annoying and sometimes dangerous threats to our airspace. The main problem is that drones are remote controlled, and too few of their pilots have earned their wings.

I know all about it from my youth, when I'd spend many a happy hour watching grown men operate remote controlled hobby boats in the Marquette Park lagoon on Chicago's South Side. They'd gas up their boats, grab their remotes, and then send 'em ripping.

It was a wondrous sight. Men with their pants legs rolled up would wade in the lagoon with hand-held remotes the size of toasters, guiding their screeching, exhaust-belching hobby boats across the water. Tiny rooster tails rose up behind them, the boats I mean, until about mid-lagoon where they'd sputter out and quit.

Cursing like hobby boat sailors, the men would use fishing rods with rubber balls attached to their lines to try and snag their boats and reel them back to shore. Typically, the fishing rods saw a lot more action than the remotes, causing me to vow then and there that when I grew up, I would not fish for boats.

And I've kept my word, though I love fishing from them, if it weren't for the distraction of the new threat now hovering and buzzing overhead, just waiting to take over my job. According to *E&P*, the FAA is poised to announce new regulations for drones that will make operating them cheaper than paying for me.

But you don't have to take my word for it. Just ask Matt Schroyer, who was interviewed for the article in *E&P*.

"According to Matthew Schroyer, executive director of dronejournalism.org, the FAA is preparing to announce new regulations for drones that would change licensing requirements, from having to acquire a pilot's license (which can cost $3,000-$4,000), to only needing to pass a knowledge test."

Who knew you needed a pilot's license to own and operate a drone? Someone had better tell the internet really soon, because there are ads for drones all over the place. To prove my point, I personally got as far as checkout for a Sky King Quadrone with Camera at J.C. Penney, and NEVER GOT CARDED for my pilot's license.

Like I would actually buy my competition. It didn't even have an attachment for carrying my notepad. But if you think it is annoying having a reporter jump up in front of you to snap your child's photo at Head Start graduation, causing you to snap a photo of the reporter's butt, imagine life in the future with Reporter Drone on duty, piloted by a kid who'd just passed his knowledge test:

- You hear buzzing overhead during a benefit dinner, swat at a fly, and drop Reporter Drone into your plate of spaghetti.

- The high school basketball game you're watching goes into overtime, and the winning basket is accidentally blocked by Reporter Drone.

- Reporter Drone stalls out and goes down in the water at the Kids Fishing Derby—and the kids refuse to cast for it!

Lucky for me, I report in a community that has way too much respect for its air space to allow Reporter Drone in. And I'll try to watch my back during Head Start graduation, too.

Laptop's Last Days

I am operating in crisis mode, because my laptop is trying to retire before me.

I have no one to blame but myself. I used my laptop to type that my working days are numbered. Its electronic ears perked up, it dropped the ball in dismay, and has been eating my homework ever since.

Maybe it is afraid I will no longer be able to pay its power bill, or pick up the tab for its occasional tune-ups. Either way, this is no time for an old dog to be playing new tricks on its owner.

The first sign of trouble happened two weeks back. I wrote a long and detailed county board story, finishing late at night. I saved it and shut my laptop with a self-satisfied snap, planning to pull up the story again in the morning, polish it up, and email it in to the office.

The next morning I warmed up with a game of online solitaire. Then I really felt the heat when I tried to bring up my story and my laptop replied: *Unsupported file, unable to retrieve.*

First, I restarted my heart. Second, I frantically punched in every possible command I knew, along with some that I made up, to try and get my story back.

Finally, I faced the truth. My dirty dog of a laptop had eaten my homework.

It was, of course, the finest piece I'd ever written. If they awarded trophies for county board stories, I'd have a second one to round out my collection (Otter Lake Ice Fishing Derby, 2nd Place) (not that I'm bragging).

As it turns out, my rewrite was good practice for the following week, when I once again put my trust in technology and got bit. This time it was my column that went off the radar, leading to another long night of chest thumping, fevered commanding, and ultimately, rewriting.

The good news is, the experience has taught this old dog a few new tricks, too.

Computers are like highway systems. There are many different ways to get from point A to point B. I can never reclaim the literary triumphs I have lost, but I've learned to avoid the potholes that swallowed them.

I still use Word Imperfect because it is a classic (ancient) program and we seniors need to stick together. I know how it feels to lose things. It feels like another late night in front of my failing laptop.

Let me tell you how I cope.

About halfway through my writing, I clasp my hands and pray my words don't go away again. Then I pry them apart to copy, paste, attach, embed, and then email my work back to myself. When I finish the story, I do it all over again, then send it in to the newspaper, too.

The road is long, almost as long as my emails, but the payoff is great: retirement someday and a place in the sun, right next to a rectangular mound of sand that looks suspiciously like someone buried their lap---

Unsupported file, unable to retrieve.

6. SNOW HAPPENS

Getting Testy About Weather

Sometimes I question peoples' intelligence.

I question it with a pop quiz! I try to trip up others so that I will feel better about being edged out as high school valedictorian by roughly half my classmates. Maybe it was two-thirds. I was not so hot at math, either.

If there is one thing I am very good at, please inform me of it soon, maybe as an early Christmas present. In the meantime, welcome to my tripper-upper titled, "A Quiz For All U.P. Seasons, Which Are Mostly Winter."

It was inspired by Joe Phillips of the National Weather Service, who told me just last week about a Colorado low. This of course brought to mind "Colorado Rocky Mountain High" by John Denver, but before I had a chance to burst into the song, Phillips had wisely moved on.

The experience left me feeling kind of testy, because my guitar was right down the hall and I think I even have the music, so I am testing you. The good news is, you don't have a grade it can affect. The better news is, I didn't have time to prepare an accompanying soundtrack.

Please clear your desk and take out a sharpened no. 2 pencil. Circle the answer that is most likely true, even if you seriously doubt it. See answers at the end, followed by a merciless grading scale (I am feeling better about myself already!).

And, begin:

1. Colorado low—A. high pressure system B. how Colorado felt when John Denver died C. work boots, low rise

2. blizzard—A. Dairy Queen treat B. heavy snow, freezing temps, high winds C. good name for a St. Bernard

3. frost—A. famous poet B. ice crystals C. what you do with cake

4. frostbite—A. how we feel about frost B. frozen body tissue C. assault by famous poet

5. flurries—A. Frosty the Snowman's offspring B. McDonald's Blizzards C. light snow

6. cold snap—A. sudden wintry weather B. processing frozen peas C. how football is handed to quarterbacks in the U.P.

7. Alberta clipper—A. Canadian barber B. Canadian boat C. fast-moving weather system

8. drift—A. wind-driven snow B. laundry detergent C. what cars do on black ice

9. black ice—A. new Marvel villain B. transparent road ice C. good name for craft beer

10. freezing point—A. when Sr. Anita used to call on me in math B. 32 degrees C. 33 ?

11. gale—A. winds 32 mph or more B. Eilola, of Pelkie C. Crystal, of country music

12. pank—A. to discipline B. what dyslexic pirates walk C. Yooper-speak for banking snow against a house as added insulation

13. sleet—A. Black Ice's evil sidekick B. wintertime target shooting C. ice pellets

14. Fahrenheit—A. not too short, not too tall B. Celsius in English C. temp scale

15. snow day—A. good reason to teach B. no school C. November through April in U.P.

Answers

1-A, 2-B, 3-B, 4-B, 5-C, 6-A, 7-C, 8-A, 9-B, 10-A or B, 11-A, 12-C, 13-C, 14-C, 15-B

Grading scale

13-15 meteorologist

10-12 weather man or woman

0-9   you're a snowflake

Kids Cure Global Warming

If you think you alone can do nothing about global warming, you clearly don't have crayons in your freezer.

That's right. At this very moment, at an undisclosed location that is actually our house in Watton, the seeds of a snow day have been planted and are fully expected to bear fruit by morning.

The power is being wielded by tiny children. They are brimming with faith, hope, and a strong desire to stay home from school tomorrow so they can play in the snow. According to my sources, which are my grandchildren, they've discovered the secret formula for making that dream come true.

As a hardened journalist brimming with skepticism, cynicism, and a touch of a cold I got from my sources, I initially wrote it off. I think I know fake news when a grandchild is telling it. Besides, I'd already heard that song and dance from their slightly older cousins last winter.

You know, the winter the kids had more snow days than school days? And the Michigan Legislature had to convene between storms to pardon school children from an extended sentence, I mean "school year," due to days missed?

A light just went on! It was the kids opening the freezer door to stuff more crayons in! Also, my writer's instinct tuning into a dangerous pattern, compelling me to warn the unsuspecting public that we are on the brink of another ice age.

I only wish this news was fake.

The threat was delivered by five-year-old Tullia, who beamed up at me shortly before her bedtime last night and announced, "I'm going to make a snow day!" Recalling the horror that was last winter, I told her, "Oh no you're not!", causing her to smile even wider and coo, "Oh yes I am!"

We went back and forth until I got bored and lost by default. Flush with victory, she proceeded to share the secret formula for making a snow day, previously known only by every other kid in the school system and a few teachers who will try anything to dodge cold germs for a day.

It sounded chillingly familiar, like the song "Muskrat Love" by Captain & Tennille. I'm sorry I just got that song stuck in your head, but it is not nearly as disturbing as the following snow day recipe the kids might be cooking up right now in your very own home:

1.   Before going to bed, flush ice cubes down the toilet.

2.   Put your pajamas on inside out.

3.   Put some crayons in the freezer, and to seal the deal,

4.   Do a snow dance.

It was a chilling revelation. At the risk of ending her innocence, I gently warned the child it works best when bad weather is actually forecast, but she was on a mission. Lacking ice cubes, she made tiny square snowballs and flushed those instead.

Her mother even hopped onboard and buttoned her three-year-old brother, Emmett, into his Paw Patrol pajamas, turned inside-out. Then both kids tucked crayons into the freezer, using colors they didn't like because there's no sense in throwing good crayons after bad weather.

I had a hand in helping choreograph the snow dance, but only because I have a strong background in utter nonsense. There was graceful arm movement to indicate strong wind, fluttering fingers to represent snow falling and fancy footwork to avoid tripping over my fellow snow dancers.

The truth will out tomorrow morning when the kids wake up to clear skies and a thermometer nudging 20 degrees, but snow day success is inevitable. Armed with the secret formula, we adults can at least stem the tide if this year's snow banks and snow days suspiciously start piling up.

Take the crayons out of the freezer, and just to be on the safe side, I'll repeat my snow dance in reverse.

Fake News? We Wish!

"It's the first day of September," I informed my husband.

"Winter's comin'," he grumbled.

Then I clocked him.

Actually, I clocked him at 15 mph, because he was behind the wheel as we were approaching the Ishpeming roundabout. The new intersection requires intense concentration, or you'll become the star of lunch or dinner theater for patrons at the Pizza Hut on the corner.

"Ooh, that was a bad one! Pass me a napkin, will ya?"

The roundabout is not the problem. Neither are the patrons, though some can be a bit judgy. No, the problem was that he was right, because it says so right in *The Old Farmer's Almanac*. Hold onto your vehicle's "oh s—" handle, even outside the Ishpeming roundabout, because we're in for it again.

Last winter was so cold and snowy, senior citizens couldn't even complain about winters being worse when they were kids. So they grumbled about modern snow days instead. Five locations in the Keweenaw Peninsula were buried under 300 inches of snow. Fortunately, our own Baraga County wasn't one of them.

That isn't necessarily good for winter tourism, but it set just fine with us residents. What didn't set well was the late February blizzard that hammered the entire Upper Peninsula, with Baraga County included in the target.

Businesses closed because their entrances were drifted-in. Schools were already closed from the last storm, so they just stayed that way. At work, I rested my camera against an upstairs window to snap a photo of a front end loader digging out our entrance below.

The glass was quite chilly. I think I felt a draft.

The grandchildren will love that story of personal suffering someday! I think they've already heard it, multiple times! And I don't care!

What I do care about is the fact that people are already complaining about the onset of this coming winter, and we still have three weeks left of summer. They are shaking in their sneakers, posting photos of last winter's whiteouts.

Worst of all, *The Old Farmer's Almanac* has got their backs.

The Old Farmer's Almanac is an American institution. It is a small yellow booklet that occurs naturally in book racks at Tractor Supply and Fleet Farm stores, and unnaturally pretty much everywhere else that books and magazines are sold.

Published annually since 1818, it provides long-range weather predictions, planting tips, and short articles, mostly of an agricultural nature. It was originally intended to help farmers, but has since been picked up by the general public and errant columnists. We can only hope the prediction for this winter is fake news.

The Old Farmer's Almanac predicts this winter's temperatures will be below normal. Snowfall will be above normal. The term "parade of snowstorms" reared its ugly head. So did the promise that in the U.P., winter will once again slop over into spring, guaranteeing yet another white Easter.

If there is one thing we Upper Michiganders are good at, it's making snow cones out of snow balls. Also, adult-flavored slushy drinks, which will clearly be needed if *The Old Farmer's Almanac* hits its average success rate of over 80 percent for weather predictions.

Even if it isn't fake news, it's old news in the U.P. where stoicism and adult-flavored slushy drinks both serve us well. And when worse comes to worse again, I'll be the first to raise my naturally frosted glass in a toast to the bitter truth.

"Here's to spring! Winter's comin'! And quick, grab that booth facing the roundabout!"

There's No Place Like Florida

It's snow season in the U.P., and we all need to learn how to walk again.

I'll bet you thought I was going to type "drive." It's a fair assumption to make as you wait for the wrecker to come pull you out of the ditch, but I feel the annual relearning how to drive theme has been vastly overdone. Besides, I'd hate to drive you over the edge when you can't even spin out of the ditch.

This public warning stems from a serious accident that nearly occurred in L'Anse just last week. It was a bright and sunny afternoon, and as I walked beneath a roof dripping melted snow, I stepped on a step. In the words of riveting Western author Louis L'Amour, "It was a real tenderfoot move."

Every hombre knows that ice forms on pavements and steps under roofs that are dripping melted snow. By mid-winter the snow is pretty well set, but you still have to keep a lookout for icicles just waiting to dry-gulch you from overhead.

I love Louis! But back to that public warning, I hit the ice, and my life flashed before my eyes. It looked just like my feet. That's because my feet were flashing before my eyes, scrambling for purchase on the icy wooden step while I channeled Curly from *The Three Stooges*.

I was on my third "Whoop!" when one foot found a dry spot and held. After a quick check for witnesses, I dove into my car and realized I needed to learn how to get into my car again, because I'd just hauled in two size 10 snowballs.

Snow s-----. If you count the dashes, you will find they stand for "sticks" instead of s----. Snow s---- because it sticks, building up in our vehicles because we forgot to unload our feet before entering.

During snow season in the U.P., you can't just climb willy-nilly into your vehicle. Mostly because nobody says willy-nilly anymore, but also because if you do, you'll have to shovel your floorboards to find your gas pedal.

From a tender age, our children are drilled on keeping snow outside the car where it belongs. Proactive parents start before the car leaves the curb at the hospital, gently tapping baby's feet together three times to pattern their newborn for success.

The rest of us just wait until the kids can walk, then holler, "Kick the tire before you get in!" The snow from their boots flies into our wheel hubs where it freezes solid, causing us to drive even more erratically but sparing us from having to shovel out the back seat to fit the kids in.

By the time they have graduated from high school, most Yoopers have mastered the universally accepted method for successful snow removal, made famous by Dorothy in the Wizard of Oz, except she lived in Kansas. For the tenderfoots among us, it goes something like this.

Open the car door and enter your vehicle backside first, leaving your snow-encased boots dangling out the door. Then smack your boots together, three times minimum, channeling Dorothy in reciting, "There's no place like Florida, there's no place like Florida, there's no place like Fl…"

7. THEY'RE ALL TEACHING MOMENTS

Working Remotely, With Children

It was the time of COVID-19, and I was watching TV from the federally approved distance of six feet because there were real, live people on the screen when singer/songwriter Keith Urban popped up, performing in his home.

Keith was performing music. Then his wife, actress Nicole Kidman, video bombed him by performing a spontaneous dance between Keith and the camera, proving she is a much better actress than dancer but a fun gal nonetheless.

The power couple was demonstrating a popular trend among professional performers of sharing your talents online—Keith a little more than Nicole—during these trying times of everyone being stuck at home with the kids.

Of course, not everybody can be a professional musician or actress, but all of us are blessed with some set of well-honed skills that might benefit our fellow man. Some are even timely. Like working with children in the home.

If there is one thing the experience has taught us, it is that we really miss seeing the school bus pull up to the house in the morning. Even more, we miss it pulling away with the kids inside because many of us are now sharing an extended spring break with them.

The main difference during these trying times is, we adults still have to do our homework. And the kids really want to help us do it.

I can't sing like Keith or act like Nicole, unless she's dancing across the room. But as a veteran writer and grandmother who regularly shares her beat with five cub reporters ages one to eight, I will happily spout off from my leaky font of wisdom. Here's a few tips for starters:

1. Establish an impenetrable workspace.

Hahaha! Sometimes I make myself laugh so hard it nearly dislodges the Cheerios stuck in my hair by the one-year-old who likes to share. You cannot lock children out. If you do, they'll put you in jail and allow the kids to visit.

I closed the bedroom door last week to do some work. The five-year-old found me, and commented on my tiny handwriting. Then she held my notes for me as I typed, swinging them around for emphasis ("SO tiny!"). Then she started talking about Oaf from the movie *Frozen,* so I had to chase her. Not a big Olaf fan.

Work while the kids sleep. They love clambering on your comatose form during daylight hours.

2. Organization is the key to success.

We have several telephones in our home. I take notes at whichever one I can get to before the grandchildren. Last week's notes were written on a sheet of yellow construction paper, the backside and front margins of a fax, and five blue Post-It notes, carefully numbered.

Always keep your pencil/crayon/eyeliner sharpened and close at hand, and by all that is holy, don't use permanent markers. They bleed right through coloring books, which are also handy for note-taking, and get you in trouble with your permanently stained co-workers' mothers.

3. Respect your co-workers.

In this busy workaday world, it is easy to forget the little people who got you where you are today, which is working at home with children. Check on your co-workers regularly. Engage them in age-appropriate projects. Challenge them to beat you to the phone.

Inquire about their day. Then do it with a British accent, like Peppa Pig. Break often to snack, read a book together, or go outside. And when the going gets tough, to quote the only line I remember from some country song, "I hope you dance."

Just like Nicole Kidman.

When working with children, it's important to remember a well fed employee is a happy one, especially when there's grapes on the table.

The Return of MEAP

A funny thing happened in town last week. Local school districts invited parents to come in and take a MEAP test.

Why do they think we grew up and got mortgages? It wasn't to get out of recess!

In case you don't know or just plain can't remember, MEAP stands for Michigan Educational Assessment Program. The MEAP test covers variations of the three Rs, and is administered to unsuspecting children whose parents callously decided to settle in Michigan.

The test used to really challenge the kids. Then students in Michigan started getting smarter and smarter, to the point where some can now fill in most of the answers before their teachers have even finished passing out the question booklets.

Of course that's an exaggeration! Nobody picks up a pencil until all booklets are passed out!

The overuse of exclamation marks above indicates a shameful attempt at avoiding messy litigation with the MEAP people. It also highlights the fact that while our children are apparently gaining ground academically, we parents are seriously slipping.

We remember the important stuff, like Christopher Columbus sailing to the New World on the Nina, the Pinta, and the Santa Maria. But if you press us for details, such as "Which boat was Christopher on?", we will scratch our noggins and guess, "Was it A?" (It was C. I Googled it).

Nobody tests you once you've graduated from school. You will have to cram for your written driver's exam every five years or so, but once you succeed in memorizing the eye chart, the rest comes easy. Income taxes challenge our grasp of basic math every spring. Unlike our school days, we can now pay people who got good grades in math to figure them out for us.

Ain't it grand being all grown up?

If your mind is starting to wander and you're becoming fatigued from holding this book at arm's length so you can read the print, I do have a point, and it's this: children who struggle with their MEAP's are still going to wildly outperform their parents, whose test scores would likely fall into the range of "Idaho potato."

And I fear, my fellow mature Michiganders, that is precisely why we have been invited to take the MEAPs.

Role reversal can be a valuable teaching tool. It teaches us humility, and helps us to appreciate the work that others do. As an added bonus, nothing is so self-affirming for our children than to have their parents squeeze into tiny desks and bomb a test they could ace in their sleep.

Schools in Baraga County offered the test on two evenings, softening the blow by promising it would only run an hour and a half and would not count toward our grade. As added incentive, coffee and cookies would be served. However, there would be no recess.

Parents could also participate at home by reviewing sample questions on MEAP's Take the Test Day link. With a little help from their Michigan student, who can find computer links easier than the laundry basket, they could ponder questions the kids encounter on a regular basis, such as:

"In our infancy, we bordered upon the Atlantic only; our youth carried our boundary to the Gulf of Mexico; today, maturity sees us upon the Pacific."--Alfred Thayer Mahan

The quote above echoes what popular belief in nineteenth century America?
A. Isolationism
B. Manifest destiny
C. States' rights
D. Separate but equal

If you answered B, you are clearly in cahoots with your Michigan student. No cookies for you.

As maturing adults we have to give credit where it's due. Our children have clearly transcended their genetic code, and Michigan has certainly raised the bar where student testing is concerned.

Now, if we could only get the kids to help us out a little with that income tax quiz next spring...

Reading Marches On

My husband recently shut down a grandchild's request to read a book.

"I can't read *Paw Patrol*," he told the tot. "It makes my head hurt."

"You can't refuse to read to a child!" I hollered from the kitchen, fortunately up to my elbows in the dishpan and therefore unable to read the wretched book. Again.

"YOU READ *PAW PATROL*!" the grandchild bellowed, stomping a Paw Patrol-slippered foot for emphasis.

They eventually reached a compromise, settling into Grandpa's recliner with an ABC book by Dr. Seuss. It's a tad predictable but has a satisfying conclusion: "I'm a zizzer zazzer zuzz, as you can plainly see."

Sorry to ruin the ending for you, but it's March is Reading Month. That means adults all over Baraga County will be heavily medicating or diving into their dishpans to survive the parade of sorry characters now starring in children's literature.

You know who you are, Rubble on the Double, Sunny Day, and Peppa Pig (though I secretly love your British accent). Also, Critter, the Berenstain Bears, and Amelia Bedelia, who really needs to lose her last name in every blooming reference.

The characters are not disturbing in themselves, unless you are the one who has to pick up after Clifford the Big Red Dog. They just keep coming back at us in the sticky little hands of our progeny who can't get enough of the same old stories.

Paw Patrol is about cartoon puppies that rescue people, basically from themselves. It is a hardcover collection of many stories including "Pup-Fu Power" and "Pup, Pup and Away!" Reading it makes my eyes bleed.

That is a blatant lie that has absolutely no place in a piece about children's literature. But honest to zizzer-zazzer-zuzz, I am compelled to read it at least three times a week because we don't have enough dirty dishes to save me.

What does save me during March and all the other reading months of the year is a decision I made long ago, post-*The Cat in the Hat* but pre-*Barbie and Skipper*. I boxed up and saved our children's books that I actually enjoyed reading, in hopes of future listeners.

Gus Was a Friendly Ghost re-emerged eight years ago, and now shares prime shelf space with *Where the Wild Things Are* and *Mr. Bell's Fixit Shop*. Beloved Golden Books, a popular series with shiny gold bindings, include *We Help Daddy*, *The Owl and the Pussycat*, and *The Little Gardeners*.

The payoff is great, right down to the tiniest grandchild who literally devours books. We just pull the pieces out of her mouth and read to her from what's left. As soon as her eye teeth come in, I'll be nudging *Paw Patrol* into her path.

In the meantime, we'll be reading anything little hands drop into our laps, no matter who/what the main character, as long as the drop is followed by a cuddle with the delivery agent. Reading educates, inspires, and entertains.

Especially when Peppa and Mummy go shopping for tomahtoes.

Setting My Record Straight

I want to start the New Year with a clean slate. The problem is, I've got a permanent record.

I got it back in 1963, when I was enrolled at Francis M. McKay elementary school on Chicago's South Side. It was a file that included my name, address, immunity record, and a note about my penchant for wearing empty eyeglass frames.

My three older brothers all wore glasses. I clearly needed some, too.

Having already established myself as a standout student, I quickly learned the importance of staying under the radar. I learned it the day we exhausted our kindergarten teacher's patience before it was even nap time.

"If you all don't behave," Mrs. Haberichter warned, "it will go on your permanent record."

Somebody, probably one of the perpetrators, asked what that was. In a solemn voice she usually reserved for reciting Five Little Jack-O-Lanterns and herding us through fire drills, Mrs. Haberichter delivered our first life lesson.

"It is a record of all the bad things you do, and it follows you through all your years in school."

We were scared straight. I vowed then and there to never again cheat at Doggy Doggy Where's Your Bone. Also, to avoid the principal's office like it was the boy's bathroom.

For the most part, I succeeded. There were warnings along the way, mostly because I tend to be chatty, but I always shut my yap on command. Like other children of the sixties, I knew that if I got in trouble at school, far harsher punishment would await me at home.

My permanent record remained pristine until one fateful day in sixth grade when I got sloppy about the rules. I left my gym suit stuffed in my locker in favor of my stylish brown corduroy jumper. Our gym teacher, Mr. Haas, who rarely even noticed, called me out on it.

I was lined up with three other stylish girls and marched off to the principal's office where we sat out the period in despair. My shame was complete when my very favorite teacher, Ms. Shore, spotted me on the office bench and exclaimed, "NANCY?"

I had hit rock bottom. Worse yet, my permanent record would forever show I didn't dress for gym day.

The problem is that over 50 years later, I've still got that blight on my background. What if I someday choose to run for public office? You know how relentless reporters can be! The headlines alone would kill my campaign:

Besonen's already been in office
Gym rat wants to represent you
She didn't even need glasses!

The answer was clear. The first thing Monday morning, I called McKay to finally clean my slate. When the secretary in the principal's office answered, I got straight to the point: whatever became of my permanent record?

"Your permanent WHAT?" she asked.

We had a nice chat, during which she said she'd never heard the term before but figured it probably existed, because "If you want to change schools and you were bad in first grade and you're still bad in seventh, well, who wants that?"

My point exactly. With the principal busy in a meeting and neither one of us willing to interrupt, we agreed that my permanent record probably didn't go any farther than McKay.

However, if I ever do decide to run for public office, let the record show my eyeglasses now have lenses.

8. IS INSECTICIDE *WRONG*?

Battling Bugs

There has never been a sequel to one of my columns, probably because there was little reason for the original. But when a concerned reader called last week to inform me she had a follow-up to one I'd written about bugs, I just had to head straight to her home to find out, "Why?"

Most people in the U.P. consider insects a nuisance, but in her bug-blurred view they are The Enemy. The battle lines were drawn right after as she moved into her home. Her personal war with all things insect has been raging ever since.

"When we first put the siding on our house, the cluster flies came," she said. "This whole house was one massive wall of flies. I immediately started studying flies."

And what did she learn?

"There are a lot of flies," she deadpanned. "I'd never come across this amount of flies. And I wasn't willing to accept it."

The cluster fly is a non-biting insect that winters in the high reaches of homes along with several thousand of its closest friends and relatives. During the spring hatch, she said, the ground fairly quivers with hatching larvae. Soon after, larvae bore into unsuspecting earthworms to feed and grow.

And what comes of the worms?

"I don't know," she said, then briskly moved on to deer flies. They are biting insects that like to attack from above, but are easily deceived. Armed with the intel, she has devised three no-fail lines of defense.

First, carry a fern while you walk and hold it high. Most deer flies will circle the fern and ignore the person waving it. If one forgets the rules, she said, you can whap it with your decoy.

Second, wear a hat, preferably one with a high profile, to draw deer flies up and away. And last but not least, the woman suggested (and she was only half kidding here) that "You should walk with a tall person."

Chemical warfare may go against the Geneva protocol, but it's fair game vs. bugs, especially in the form of natural "Stiky Stuff." The glue-like substance is effective on several fronts, and the woman has become downright devious in her generous application.

She led the way to her basement for a live demonstration. She tore off a sheet of aluminum foil and poured a small puddle of Stuff in the middle. She spread it with a paint brush, molded the sticky foil around an old cake pan and, voila! Unhappy landings for guests who are pests.

Back in the light of day, she pointed out Stuff-covered bleach jugs strung like Japanese lanterns between her trees. There were more around her garden and orchard, and strips of fabric spread with Stuff hung from her screen door, all set to trap unwanted guests.

Her favorite weapon is an original design that will never go out of fashion. It's a straw hat liberally painted with Stiky Stuff for attacking the flying insect problem head-on. The woman said she's already blackened three hats so far this summer, just working in her yard and garden.

The war is far from over, but she feels she's gaining ground in her battle with bugs. You can join in by contacting Olson Products of Ohio for your own artillery. In the meantime, wear a hat, wave a fern, and encourage your tall friends to hold their heads high.

Don't Run With Spiders

If you are a fan of the *Eentsy Weentsy Spider* or *Charlotte's Web*, turn the page quick because I am about to stomp all over your hero in print.

Still with me? Welcome to the club, and if my exhaustive research (two websites) serves me well, we are not alone in our aversion to spiders. There is even a name for our delicate condition. It's called "sensible."

No it's not! It's arachnophobia, and it's the most common phobia in the Western culture because spiders have got us surrounded. They can be found on every continent except Antarctica and in every habitat not counting the air and the deep blue sea.

I am already doubting one of my websites, because I have personally witnessed spiders inhabiting the air. They love to dangle from a strand of their web in a fun game they call, "Fishing for arachnophobes." They are also seaworthy, stowing away on boats to populate foreign lands unless they are Antarctica.

While spiders everywhere are busy plotting their next fishing trip or ocean cruise, let's take a look at why people find them so scary. Prepare to be very afraid.

Sit down at your computer and type "Spider Identification Chart—Venomous or Dangerous?" in the search engine. Now scroll down to the picture of the Huntsman spider. Tap it with your cursor... wait for it... and... IT WIGGLES ON YOUR SCREEN! Like an arachnophobe needs to see that!

It's nice to know the scientific community has a sense of humor. I hope it receives a fresh shipment of bananas real soon from a foreign country where the wiggling Huntsman spider is particularly prevalent, and has vacation time to burn.

The thing about bugs is, they don't ordinarily bug me. I swat mosquitoes, squish gnats, and pluck wood ticks off my hide without batting an eye. The thing about spiders is, they're not bugs. As soon as one hops aboard, I'm up on my feet, giving the entire cast of River Dance a run for its money.

Most people who suffer from a phobia go out of their way to avoid facing what they fear. Luckily for me, I am not averse to spontaneous bouts of Irish step dancing. And thanks to a web that would have put Charlotte to shame, I put on quite the performance in our woods last week.

I enjoy walking in the woods. If the mood is right or the bugs are thick, I enjoy running. The thing about running in the woods is, you have to keep your eyes on the ground to avoid tripping. That leaves you wide open for racing straight into spider webs.

The one I hit last week was loaded for bear. It was tightly strung between two trees on either side of a wide path, and was so strong I could literally hear it rip away as it clung tightly to my face, arms, and t-shirt.

I now know how a lake trout feels in a gill net. I tore off my baseball cap and swiped at the web, hopping and hollering while hoping the spider wasn't attached to me too. If so, I guarantee his first rodeo ride was a short one.

Later that same night, I was reading in bed when I felt something on my arm, like a strand of hair that had fallen out from all that dancing. I turned a page, brushed it off, then looked down to see it was actually a big daddy long legs, now delicately picking its way across my bedspread.

All God's critters got a place in the choir, and that particular spider is now singing in several sections. It just seemed like the sensible thing to do.

Targeting Ticks

In my ongoing effort to prevent the U.P. from becoming overpopulated, I pay homage each summer to one native bug that truly lives up to its name.

Dishonorees have included but are not limited to the mighty mosquito, nasty old gnats, and the always politically incorrect *no-see-um*. In honor of the blighter my husband plucked off my back tonight, this year I am targeting wood ticks.

Wood ticks are flat little bugs that attach themselves to wild and domestic animals and suck their blood until they ask their husbands, "Is there something on my back?" They also spread diseases including Rocky Mountain spotted fever and Lyme disease.

As I wait to break out in spots and/or lymes, allow me to explain to our now captivated U.P. guests. The U.P. is usually snow covered and slippery. When the snow finally goes away, gnats come out, followed by mosquitoes, ticks, and no-see-ums.

Oh, and we also have wolves and bears.

Sorry, realtors! I'm just trying to avoid having to wait in long lines at the co-op. Wood ticks can be found anywhere on humans, but in nature they prefer to cling to tall grass, waving all their little arms in hopes of latching onto an unsuspecting passer-by.

After they've succeeded in transferring to their meal ticket, they hide in wait for just the right opportunity to crawl across the landscape and dig in. Wood tick bites are usually painless, and often go undetected until their host suddenly realizes that her mole has eight legs.

I am seeing the light through the co-op line already.

The preferred method for removing a wood tick is to grasp it with a tweezers close to the point of entry and pull upward with steady, even pressure. You should never crush a tick between your fingers. Instead, put it in alcohol, a sealed bag or container, or flush it down the toilet.

The usual way to remove a wood tick is to grab the bug by its flat little body and pluck hard. If you have your pocket knife handy, give it the ol' Anne Boleyn. If not, just use your ax. In either case, clean the bite site. I like to add a dab of generic Neosporin for good measure.

Now that I have literally scared the pants off my readers (check under your shirt, too), I would like to lighten the mood by ending with a cute little joke about wood ticks. It is my all-time favorite.

A Yooper hosting a friend from Texas took him for a ride in the woods, hoping to spot some native wildlife. To his delight, a magnificent eight point buck bounded across the road in front of them.

"Where I come from, we call that a yearling," the Texan drawled.

Shortly after, the Yooper was thrilled when they spotted a black bear, close to 300 pounds, poised by a log at the edge of a clearing.

"Nice cub," the Texan said with a yawn.

The Yooper was steaming mad by now, and continued the ride in silence, until they happened upon a huge snapping turtle laying its eggs in the gravel beside the road.

The Texan jumped up in his seat, pointed and bellowed, "What's that?!"

His host cast a bored look over at the snapper and replied, "Wood tick."

Beetles Ain't No Ladybugs

Ladybug, ladybug, fly away home. Your house is on fire. I know, because I lit it.

If you think that is a bit harsh, you do not have two ladybugs currently circling your head, bouncing off the light fixture between passes. They are frantically searching for the third member of their party, who is busy reading the label inside my shirt collar.

U.P. residents, like biblical peoples of yore, are no strangers to plagues. They had locusts. We have mosquitoes. They had boils. We scratch until we infect. They got religion. We've still got ladybugs.

Three summers ago, armies of tent worms invaded the land and stripped our trees of foliage and fruit. We countered the attack by wrapping tin foil around our trees, resulting in continued defoliation but better TV reception.

Then winter came, and the worms disappeared.

The following summer, big fat flies came to pass and ate the baby tent worms. Then they wiped their faces on whatever was hanging on the clothesline, begetting stubborn stains and cries of "Ee-yew!" across the land.

Then winter came, and the flies disappeared.

Last summer, after purchasing hefty insurance policies against home fires, swarms of ladybugs packed their bags and descended upon the U.P. They congregated by the entry ways, and every time a door opened, they shoved another little dotted gal in.

Winter has returned, and the ladybugs are still bugging us.

Where did the ladybugs come from? What do they eat? Why are they still here? And most important of all, how do you make your fingers quit stinking after pinching one of them to an early grave?

A short cruise on the internet reveals there are literally hundreds of different types of ladybugs, all dressed basically the same. Upon closer scrutiny, it would appear the little culprit currently doing the backstroke in my coffee cup is not a lady at all, but a Mexican bean beetle.

The beetle is brownish-orange in color, lighter if you use cream. If you have bifocals or young children, you can use them to confirm it has eight small black spots in three rows across its shell. Its larvae, when magnified on the internet, could make a grown man scream.

The Mexican beetle can be found almost anywhere in the U.S. It feeds on a variety of beans including that U.P. staple, green beans. Alfalfa, clover, cowpea, or kudzu also go down smooth. It can cause extensive crop damage, but only in areas that boast extensive crops. Score one for the U.P.

Mexican bean beetles are reputed to "overwinter underneath litter and other rubbish in hedgerows, ditches, banks, and woods." If you have one reading over your shoulder right now, it does not bode well for your housekeeping skills.

The most disturbing fact is that Mexican bean beetles have large families. Very large families. We are talking 460 offspring in the course of one fun-filled summer. What is a beetle-plagued population to do?

Make sudden and unannounced vacuum sweeps. Change the bag often to prevent your untimely asphyxiation by dead beetle bodies. Repeat daily until spring when, in the spirit of the song, "There was an old lady who swallowed a fly," the U.P. is visited upon by yet another plague.

We're hoping for frogs this time. They make great bait.

Tiniest, Mightiest Predator

Before embarking upon my annual lapse of good judgment that is a week of vacation at Fish Camp, I present a short but terribly relevant quiz:

Q: What blight upon the U.P.'s summer landscape causes full-grown adults to speak as if they were starring in a Spaghetti Western?

A: No-see-ums.

Surely you've seen Spaghetti Westerns. Clint Eastwood developing his broodiness? Native Americans speaking like non-natives put bad words in their mouths? No? Well, you haven't seen no-see-ums either, but we've all felt the sting.

I met my first no-see-um shortly after arriving in the U.P. from my native Chicago. I felt a sharp sting on my arm, slapped myself sillier, and found I had just dispatched a grain of pepper. A welt rose, and when I asked a fellow reporter for his medical opinion, I was told, "No-see-um."

"Whaddaya' mean, you no-see-um? It's right there! And it's itchy!"

I learned to wear long sleeves year-round, and to shut our windows when the sun went down, even if the summer heat was still up. But for those who seek real answers to U.P. life's littlest mysteries, I give you: Wikipedia!

According to the source that is just slightly sketchier than me, no-see-ums are small, bloodsucking insects. They are members of the big, happy Ceratopogonidae family. It includes biting midges averaging 1-4 mm tall, proving good things don't always come in small packages.

Wikipedia doesn't say where the no-see-um name comes from. Possibly the same person who named the Wampum Shop in Mercer, WI, where I will soon be perusing the cedar box section for a cheap Fish Camp souvenir. They even have tiny fly swatters for no-see-ums, but the boxes are more practical.

Female no-see-ums are the only bloodsuckers of the bunch, feeding so they can settle down and raise a family of babies they can't see. Male no-see-ums are too busy trying to find no-see-um women to bother with the rest of us.

The bugs bite like mosquitoes, but their sting can prove even worse. The welt they raise is actually an allergic reaction to proteins in their saliva. Besides being practically invisible and able to attack us right through a screen, they are also messy eaters.

They lay their eggs under bark, in rotten wood, compost areas, etc. which basically describes the U.P. landscape. Some tropical species have regular day jobs as important pollinators of crops like cacao. In the U.P., the bums just hang out and attack us.

There are several steps you can take to protect yourself from no-see-ums. The most obvious is to retreat, screaming and scratching at the grains of pepper latching onto you, until the bugs spot the "Welcome to Illinois" sign and run for their lives.

In the evenings, when the little vampires really stretch their wings, you can shut every window in the house and turn off the lights, which also attract no-see-ums. It will plunge you into darkness and quite possibly despair, but at least you won't itch.

If you do feel the sting, the welt may last as long as a week, though it can be soothed with a topical antihistamine. The good news is, relief is just a few short months away when snow brings an end to the reign of the U.P.'s tiniest, mightiest predator.

I, however, will be back in one short week spouting a fresh batch of non-sense-um from Fish Camp. And maybe a little cedar box from the Wampum Shop, too.

9. AGING GRACELESSLY

It's All Gray Area

When I was younger, I knew all the answers. Now that I'm older, I just wish I'd written them down.

Everything is black and white when you are knee high to authority. You like cookies. You love Princess Anna in "Frozen." Ergo, not to be confused with Olaf, if a box of cookies has her picture on the front, you must have it. Right Now!

If adults shopped like children, our carts would be loaded with items featuring our favorite characters, like raspberry J.Lo and frozen Brad Pittzas. And that would just be disturbing, with the obvious exception of Reese's Witherspoon Pieces.

The problem with growing up is that everything, including me, is gray area.

As a high school freshman, I knew as a fact that I didn't need to learn algebra because I'd never need it. Whoever invented algebra was a real ding dong. (Spot quiz: which famous face would sell the most Ding Dongs in America today? Spot answer: any Kardashian).

As a senior citizen, I realize I needed to learn high school algebra so that I wouldn't drag my GPA any deeper into the gutter. My elusive mastery of the accursed subject would also have made Algebra I with Sr. Anita a lot less scary.

Math was a problem that my mind, geared more toward English, just could not comprehend. For example, adding negatives made no sense to me because regardless of the formula, you always wound up with nothing anyway.

Then I grew up and learned the gray area. College tuition plus room & board made me permanently park my '67 Chrysler Newport because I couldn't afford both a degree and wheels. Algebraically speaking, $ct + r\&b = bus$.

When I was young, I knew as a fact that I had freedom of speech. I learned it in my U.S. Government class. And that was about all I learned in U.S. Government, because immediately after, I closed my book and got busy yakking.

I loved my freedom of speech! I practiced it regularly! I drove my teachers nuts, except for Sr. Anita who always had my number. Then I became a high school senior, and learned the gray area: my rights end where another person's begin.

The lesson was driven home the day our high school rings came in. It was a sacred tradition at Maria High School on Chicago's South Side that on Senior Ring Day, the seniors were dismissed early to celebrate, I don't know, new jewelry.

Girls who were blessed with cars would load them up with their fellow classmates, then drive around the neighborhood, expressing their freedom of speech by laying on their horns. Heavily.

There was just one little problem. Maria High School's founding mothers had thoughtlessly built right next door to Holy Cross Hospital.

After years of peeling their patients off the ceilings on Senior Ring Day, the hospital finally shut us down. Our class, the very "Spirit of '76," had to finish out the day in school. Freely speaking, I wrote the obvious solution, right in my Senior English class journal:

"For crying out loud, they're already in the hospital. Just give them more drugs!"

And to think Mom had wanted me to go into nursing.

If I may still speak freely, I actually had all the answers from my youth, clearly recorded in bold blue Bic. I threw them away. My kids didn't need to be reading that in their mother's Senior English class journal.

Better they should buy a newspaper, preferably the one she works for, and help her keep those negatives in check.

Glasses for Fashion

I wore glasses while writing my Christmas cards this year. Not that I need to wear glasses. I was just making a fashion statement.

A lot of people make fashion statements in their mid-40s. I started early, at five years old. That was when every single person in our family wore glasses except me. My eyes were fine, but in my heart of hearts, I really wanted glasses.

I possess the foolish ability to cross my eyes, and I used it to try to convince my kindergarten teacher that I was in severe ocular distress. Focusing on my nose, I would tug at her sleeve and inform her, "Mrs. Haberichter, I need glasses!"

Mrs. Haberichter had a lot to deal with back then including bloody noses, projectile vomiting, and Eggbert the Easter Eggs that wouldn't shut tight. But she was clearly stumped by a kid who couldn't see straight. I could see it in both her concerned faces.

So she sent me to the sick bench, where I whiled away the afternoon watching two of every student play Red Rover Red Rover Let This Dog Come Over. I was benched for three full days before Mrs. Haberichter finally phoned home.

I had a history of peculiarity, but Mom hauled me off to the eye doctor anyway. I read the doctor's eye charts with the accuracy of an Air Force Pilot, then skipped into the waiting room to pick out my frames. While I was gone, he gave Mom some sage advice:

"The circus is in town. Sell her cheap."

No he didn't! But she couldn't afford pricey psychiatric counseling, either, so instead they decided upon a wise and wonderful solution. Mom bought a cheap pair of sunglasses at the dime store, popped out the lenses, and perched the empty frames on my freckled nose.

The gift of vision is a wondrous thing, and I never sat the sick bench again. Mom said that one day we were halfway to school when I realized I'd left my glasses at home. My eyes dove straight for my nose and stayed there until she hauled us four kids back home and snagged my frames off the table.

I don't remember that, but I do recall that just two years ago, justice finally prevailed. On my second trip to the eye doctor in 40-some years, the optometrist pulled a machine in front of my face and miraculously unblurred the eye chart I'd been misreading.

"You need glasses," he announced.

"I'd like a second opinion."

"O.K. (pause) You need glasses."

There is nothing like repetition to drive a message home, and scarcely a week later I had that old familiar feeling on my nose. If I looked through the top half of my new glasses, I could see distances just fine. If I looked through the bottom half, I could read. If I looked at the line in between, I slammed into walls.

I wore them religiously at first, but felt awfully conspicuous sporting frames that had lenses. It was a big bother looking up to see traffic signals and down to read romances, and if I so much as touched a lens, my world was reduced to a big fat blur again.

On the upside, I could glare over the tops of my glasses at the children. I could whip them off for emphasis, and polish them as I pondered the answer to a difficult question. I'd gone to the eye doctor for a touch of farsightedness, and come home as F. Lee Bailey.

With glasses comes wisdom, and I have decided I am not quite ready for full-time wear. I do not need glasses to write, because I use my laptop, which can somehow be programmed to spit out letters the size of new potatoes. Our blurry blond kid is real handy at that.

I no longer worry about what it says on aspirin bottles. I medicate on faith alone. If I can fully extend my arm without injuring my neighbor, I can read without my glasses. If the person in the pew in front of me holds his or her hymnal up and to the side, I can even sing.

The glasses are within fumbling distance for reading in the morning and late at night. They're also handy for writing checks and Christmas cards. When I see my optometrist again this summer, I'll thank him for his opinions, then share one of my own: I think I need a little stronger fashion statement.

I was too "rad" to learn to knit as a child, much to my mom's dismay. Her legacy lives on in the great grandchild who wraps her yarn around knitting needles, not fish hooks.

I'm So Rad

I remember it as if it were yesterday.

Actually, I remember it as if it were the '70s, which in the neighborhood of my brain occupies much better real estate. The '70s were "rad," which was short for radical. We were so radical we didn't even finish our words.

Forty years later, kids still cut their vocabulary short, but I am no longer rad. I learned it a couple years ago from the girl at the drug store who rang up my purchases, smiled at me, and loudly asked, "Did you find everything OK, Hon?"

First, I need to emphasize we were not in the deep South, where everyone is Hon unless they are Sugar. If you can't find anything nice to say about someone in the South, you say "Bless her heart." I learned that from my BFF, Sue. She's rad, too.

Second, I was not purchasing prescription drugs for myself. They were for my mother. The peanut M&M's were for me, because I am so young at heart.

I grabbed up my bag and went out in a huff—the girl probably thought my sugar was a little low—and would have forgotten the whole uncool scene if it wasn't for that rerun at a gas station a short time after. That girl asked, "Which pump, Hon?"

So I ran her down. Ha ha! That is what you call a "senior moment," and it's way premature because I am not even old enough to get *AARP* magazine. And that is what you call a boldface lie, but I never read *AARP* unless the senior on the cover is '70s' heartthrob Greg Brady.

That is the problem with aging in America. That, and all those scary seniors in home mortgage ads on TV. We start life darling or cute, even when we are toting a load. In the middle, we are a "looker" or "ripped." Fully mature to overripe, we're back to cute again, or worse yet, a Hon.

I saw it with my mom, a 100-pound dynamo who, at age 85, had just had major surgery. They had her up and walking, probably from the operating room back to recovery, and as she doggedly inched her walker down the corridor, a young nurse beside me gushed, "She's so cute!"

Cute? The woman had four children in five years. She'd led dens of rowdy Cub Scouts, seen two sons off to military service and back, and sponsored Dad when the slots were winning because "Sharing is caring, Kathryn." The woman was a tiger!

I didn't correct the nurse because Mom raised me better. She also loved her nurses and would have wrapped that walker right around my ears for correcting one.

Neither did I correct the kid behind the counter at McDonald's the day he asked me, way too soon, "Would you like the senior coffee?"

I might add that I was dressed especially rad that day, in my jeans that don't bag and a black t-shirt and a black jacket. The ensemble looks kind of Johnny Cash-y, but black is very figure flattering, especially when you are starting to gather moss.

Instead of asking for the manager, who was probably even younger than the kid at the counter, I leaned in and whispered, "What's the price difference?"

I have been drinking my coffee on the cheap ever since.

Remarkably, I have never been carded while requesting cheap coffee, though I'm itching to pull that trigger: "You said it first!" I guess the kids behind the counters were raised better, too.

The system still has some snags. The cup is small, like my mom, and if you order your senior coffee after 6 p.m., they automatically ask if you want decaf. I think the kids are worried that we seniors won't get our sleep and will come back even crankier tomorrow.

Bless their hearts.

Baldness a Growing Concern

If your hair is thinning or missing altogether, your baseball cap needs to get lit.

I learned about the medical miracle in a TV advertisement, which is your modern vehicle for spreading miraculous medical news. It started out with a man who was deeply concerned about his ever-spreading scalp.

He grimaced at his mirror as he parted both hairs. He tried your traditional comb-over for top coverage. Then he got mad and stormed off-screen, which left me to wonder: Do I have time to grab a snack before my show comes back on?

Before I could fulfill my role as a consumer, he was back, sporting a big smile and a baseball cap. He was smiling because making commercials is a highly lucrative occupation. Also, because his baseball cap was supposedly growing him a fresh batch of hair.

You read it right, even though it defies the laws of both nature and good fashion sense. You can now regenerate hair cells that you thought had bitten the dust, simply by wearing a baseball cap embedded with dozens of tiny laser lights.

It's like being the MVP in your very own night game! You put on the cap, which has its own battery pack (plus handy carrying case) and wear it for just six minutes a day. As they say on garden seed packets, growing zone 4, your crop will mature in about 90 days.

During your hair growing season, your laser-lit baseball cap allegedly stimulates and energizes your hair follicles. Your poor balding head, which has not even been stimulated by a comb in recent years, suddenly finds itself in the spotlight.

To its credit, the cap is engineered so that the lasers don't go on until your hat does, shielding your eyes from the harmful rays of your growing lights. Hats are available in varying watts, ranging from peach fuzz to Rod Stewart.

The commercial took me back to simpler times, not quite shave-and-a-haircut-two-bits times, but shortly after. It was back when real men shined their shoes before they left home to go to the office. And sometimes they shined their heads, too.

Head polish was the original solution for bald spots. You'd choose a color that replicated what was left of your mane, then apply it right to your scalp so that it all blended together in a lustrous mass of thinning hair and head paint.

My own dad dealt with the affliction, not so much the bald spot that he couldn't see anyway, but of my brothers, Mark and Jim. They worshiped the Three Stooges, those slapstick celebrities of simple times, and worked up a regular routine around the clearing on Dad's noggin.

Jim would open the show, sneaking up behind Dad as he sat reading the paper, then pretending to blow on the bald spot like he was fogging a pair of glasses. He'd swipe his forearm back and forth about an inch over Dad's head, pretending to buff it.

Then Mark would tag in, snapping an imaginary towel over Dad's head and pretending to polish his dome to a high-gloss shine. This was my cue to join in, fulfilling my legacy as the little sister by snitching, "Dad, the boys are polishing your head again!"

If Dad were still here, I know just the gift I'd give him this Father's Day: a baseball cap with a rear view mirror.

50 Years Young

Last weekend, I helped one of my peers mark a milestone in the course of her human development.

I sat around a table with a half dozen other adults trying to figure out which end of a kazoo to blow "Happy Birthday" into while Deb, decked out in a fuzzy pink tiara, plastic lei, and coconut shell bra (over her shirt of course), waited to blow out the candles on her Disney Princesses 50th birthday cake.

Deb has been my friend longer than I can remember. Never mind that I can't quite recall what I had for lunch yesterday. I am sure I have known Deb longer than that, because we have photos of her and her family to prove it. They are somewhere around here.

If your daddy fought in WWII and was real happy to come home to your mommy, chances are you will be blowing out 50 candles in the near future, too. Thirty used to be the banner year for birthday abuse, but in the good ol' USA the majority—as in the Medicare Generation—still rules.

As we Baby Boomers age, we keep raising the bar, just because we still can. Someday nursing homes will have to budget for kazoos and coconut bras, a direct slam to young whippersnapper administrators who are still peeved because nobody sent them a dead bouquet for their 30th birthday.

This was not at all the case for Deb, whose husband Mark and teenage son Carl pulled out all the stops to ensure she would turn 50 in style. They began by assembling an A-list of guests from points across the globe including mostly Illinois, but also Wisconsin and Michigan.

As a member of Team Michigan, my task was to lie like a rug so I could get Deb out of the house while her other guests sneaked in. I accomplished this by calling three days before the event and cleverly announcing my husband and I would be driving six hours to Madison, WI, for the day, and hey Deb! Let's go shopping when we get there!

I don't lie well unless it is fishing-related, and I'm even worse at shopping, but Deb took the bait. Soon after we arrived, I spirited her downtown where we spent three hours searching with might and main for a guitar book I already owned. Then we dug through every bargain bin at a sidewalk sale until I found just the right $3 print for our log home: "Seaside Cottage."

When we arrived back at her place, Deb wondered aloud at a strange vehicle in the driveway. By now a seasoned liar, I assured her it probably belonged to another woman with whom her husband was having a torrid affair. Then I shoved her inside and bolted for the bathroom, which is also a frequent and popular party stop for the baby booming crowd.

As I emerged, my fellow party goers were still rising from their seats to greet the guest of honor. Deb, totally taken by the deceit of those whom she trusted and loved, rose to the occasion by regally donning her tiara, lei, and the coconut contraption.

Most of her guests were friends from the small private college where she and Mark had met and earned their degrees. They shared rollicking memories from their days of academia, convincing me that so long as I live I will never, ever send one of our children there. But I wouldn't mind attending an alumni function sometime.

Swingers that we are, we moved right along to the hottest party topic for people our age: who's scheduled for surgery? When you party hearty for 50 years, your assorted parts are bound to give, including your elbow joints from hoisting all those helpings of birthday cake.

One malady led to another, and before you knew it, we were comparing medical records to see who held the shabbiest hand. Opening with arthritis, we upped the ante with high cholesterol, saw that and raised it with hypertension, and then the house went wild.

Hair loss drew several balding nods. Rheumatism struck a chord, but nobody raised a hand because we were a bit stiff from the damp weather. In the end, a hysterectomy trumped a hernia, unless you are a man, in which case a migraine beats natural childbirth. Of twins.

Before the party got too out of hand, Mark called Carl out of his hiding place upstairs to come cut the cake, because he had the steadiest hand. But first we had to guess the names of the four princesses on top, finally agreeing on Snow White, Rapunzel, Cinderella, and Pamela Anderson.

After elevating both our blood sugar and cholesterol levels to dazzling new heights, we moved the party outside where we slumped down into lawn chairs and shared yet more golden memories of growing older without actually growing up.

Then, because it was perilously close to 11 p.m., we called it a night.

Deb hugged all her guests goodbye, assuring us we are not getting better, we're just getting older. She was still waving regally as the last car pulled out of their drive, and at a final glance back, appeared to be fairly glowing.

I think it was the taillights reflecting off her tiara.

10. FOR THE HEALTH OF IT

I'm Poopeye the Sailor Mom

If you find my headline rather distasteful, you are not my son.

Sam conferred the title upon me when I showed up for a fishing trip looking like I'd just lost a bar fight. My eyes were red and swollen and clearly causing me great pain, which I was fully prepared to endure just so he could troll three more lines.

And he laughed and called me "poop eye."

The fact is, I am suffering from a serious medical condition. It's called motherhood. It causes you to produce progeny who in turn produce germs that come back to bite you right in the eyeballs. That's right. I've got me a case of conjunctivitis.

It started with the youngest grandchild, who lost the bar fight first. She thanked her mother for the gift of life by paying her conjunctivitis forward. Just as my daughter was starting to see the light of day again, I found myself crying into my pillow, and it wasn't because I'd just lost a fish.

After convincing my eyes to open the following morning, I checked the facts. There are two types of conjunctivitis, viral and bacterial, and contact with the p-word (poop!) is not the only culprit. It can also be caused by a virus, allergens, contact lenses, and grandchildren.

I may have added that last item, but as far as I can see the rest is 100 percent true. I also learned that cold compresses can help relieve pinkeye symptoms including swelling, redness, and social rejection. That's why I went spring fishing in Marquette Harbor.

Sam enjoys fishing even more than I do, if you can imagine, and fishes the harbor as soon as the ice is out. Sometimes he has to crack it himself, nudging a path through small icebergs with a beat-up oar. He might have a problem with fishing.

And it might be genetic, because Friday morning I donned my darkest sunglasses and most of my wardrobe to ply the harbor's frigid waters with my son and husband for whatever can swim through slush.

Sam drove us to the marina, and didn't even notice I was rocking the movie star look until his dad shared my dirty little secret: "Your mom's got pinkeye!" Sam was visibly shaken, and requested a visual. That's when I realized it was just the potholes that had Sam all shook up.

"Poop eye!" he hooted, smiling wide at me in his rear view mirror.

"Is not!" I hollered back, squinting in the intense brightness of his pickup truck's black interior before going all Hollywood again. "It's a medical condition!"

He did not let up. Mama didn't raise a quitter. And we held in there too, his dad and I, in a bracing 40 degrees and light north wind that was a balm for both eyes and soul. It was social distancing at its very best, unless of course you were the three Coho in our live well.

I'm already looking forward to our next fishing trip. Until then, Poopeye the Sailor Mom will be medicating with cold compresses, hold the spinach.

Besonen vs. Crowbar

It seems that every day you hear another story about someone filing a lawsuit because he or she did something stupid.

That is why I am taking our crowbar to court.

Strike that from the record! I would hate to lose my case before it even began due to an unfortunate misrepresentation of me by myself. I blame my recent head injury, which actually sounds pretty good. Add that to the record!

My case against my crowbar began when my husband (who I still might name as an accomplice—it was his crowbar, after all) told me he was going to tear apart an old deck. I offered to lend my expertise to its full extent, which amounts to pulling nails.

For the sake of the jury, I would like to explain that "pulling nails" means "pulling nails." You hammer a rusty nail poking through a gnarly board until the head pops out the other side, then flip the board over and pull the nail out with the defendant, the crowbar.

You pull rusty nails so you can use the gnarly wood for other building projects, like deer blinds. You can even re-use the rusty nails if you hammer them straight again, a practice that could potentially flood our courts with personal injury lawsuits, if they weren't already busy with Besonen vs. Crowbar.

I told my husband I'd come help him out right after I hung my load of wash. I hung the wash, had a cup of coffee, played a quick game of Yahtzee to keep my Shake of the Day skills sharpened for my upcoming Fish Camp vacation, then dutifully pedaled my bike to the work site.

I was met with all the enthusiasm a man can muster when he's trying to salvage boards from a deck assembled with sinker nails. They hold on even tighter than regular nails, I guess, and whoever built that old deck, attached to a house trailer that was even older, couldn't get enough of 'em.

I pounded, pulled, and cussed while he used his tractor bucket and sledge hammer to pry boards apart. Then I took another laundry break to hang my second load, drink more coffee, and read an article about Festive Decorations for Fall.

It steeled me for the final step, stacking the planks inside a shed so they wouldn't get even rottener. And I was doing just fine, until I came across a board with a small chunk of wood still attached. That just had to go, so I reached for the crowbar.

Working in a manner that would make OSHA shut down Michigan, I approached the job at a precarious angle and started to pry. I heard a creak. Then a louder creak. Then said crowbar did willfully, knowingly, and intentionally bonk me right on the head.

The crowbar allegedly lost its purchase, and its sharp tip rapped my forehead. I felt for a bump, and my head felt wet. Then my head began to drip. Then it dripped on my new leather work gloves and the situation turned serious.

My husband advised me to hold my head together while he drove me back to the house on our ATV. He comforted me by saying the lump would nicely match the one I still sport from trying to ride Kay MacMillan's bike with no hands when I was eight years old.

That made me bleed even harder.

The small puncture wound sealed soon after—I mean, "bled out"—and if it please the court, that is why I am seeking minimal damages in Besonen vs. Crowbar. Maybe a little Festive Decoration for Fall. Preferably without sinker nails attached.

Defender of Fat On Slippery Slope

Jack Sprat could eat no fat. I could be his little woman.

Make that "big woman," except I prefer to travel light so I can extend my ice fishing season. As you can tell, this rumination is an unapologetic celebration of all things fat, and preferably saturated.

I love fat! And butter really does make everything better. I choose my cuts of meat based on what the butcher failed to trim. When the kids threaten me with a suet ball for Christmas, I only ask that they hold the seeds.

I got my grease tooth from my dad. Mom topped her beef roasts with a slab of suet for added flavor. Dad called it "crunchy munchy" and doled it out to us kids like communion. When Mom fried cubed steaks in butter, he'd swipe her pan clean with a slice of white bread while patiently defending his unrefined cuisine.

"It's gravy bread, Kathryn."

"It's grease bread, Bob!"

Then he'd split his slice down the middle and share it with me, salted of course, starting me down a slippery slope that will someday make my gallbladder fall right through my socks. Until then, I'm all for fat and happy.

Fat defenders unfortunately fight an uphill battle in modern America, the land of the free and home of the Spanx. We can eat anything we darn well please. We're just discouraged from showing its obvious effects.

Art History 101 tells us this has not always been so. That's the college class I attended with another hundred-or-so worldly scholars in a lecture hall at Northern Illinois University. It was taught by the tiny speck that was our professor, poised beside a massive screen way down in front.

The screen was huge to accommodate cattle classes. Also, to fully display the female form as captured by 16th-century artists like Peter Paul Rubens, who equated beauty with abundance and wasn't afraid to paint it.

Rubens was a true Renaissance man whose models were women of considerable substance. His well-rounded cherubs were also off the charts, painted lolling around or hovering overhead in clear violation of future FAA weight restrictions.

More artists followed his lead, resulting in the Baroque Period and oils shortages at 16th-century paint stores. It was a wonderful chapter in human history, when big was beautiful and being thin just meant you couldn't afford to eat.

Times changed and cutbacks were inevitable, starting with women's middles which were cinched so tight they could be spanned with two hands. Many models were cut clear in half, resulting in your modern art.

Let it never be said I didn't listen in Art History 101. Let it never be said I aced it, either, but I can whip you up a piece of gravy bread that will bring a tear to your eye, a lump to your throat, and a rather uncomfortable feeling in the general area of your gallbladder.

Flu Bug Bites

Welcome to flu season. Please have a seat, and the undertaker will see you shortly.

If you think I'm once again exaggerating in print, you are among the growing minority still enjoying good health. Cherish the moment and hold your loved ones close, because the rest of us are coughing and sneezing like howitzers and we will TAKE YOU DOWN!

I wasn't always this callous. On the job last Tuesday, I was fairly skipping through the Healthy Heart Fair in Baraga, juggling my overflowing freebie bag with my camera bag as I snapped photos of people having fun learning about fitness.

Along the way I won a baggie of granola for turning in a circle five times without falling on my face, a book by the Property Brothers just for filling out a survey, and a lap robe because I spun a prize wheel and that's where it stopped.

I was flush with my good fortune. It was the best of times! And then it was the worst.

Surely God would not smite me for doing good, which is my take on Healthy Heart Fair participation. I am thinking sometime soon after the event I just inhaled when I should have exhaled, and let that stinkin' flu bug in.

By bedtime on Thursday night I was feeling feverish, with a heaviness in my chest. It was the cat lying on me. I rousted him off but the feeling lingered, like a portent of evil things to come. So I rolled over and slept on it.

The portent, not the cat, and it only got worse. Friday morning I dragged myself out the door to spend the day with my four-year-old grandson. Huddled under a blanket on the living room floor, I became a lumpy road system for a steady stream of Matchbox Car traffic.

"Gummi, I need another road!" he'd cry, and the blanket would shift with a low moan to offer a new pass over the mountain. Then a little car would swoop over my hip, making lugging noises that I felt were a bit excessive, but Gummi is not one to quibble.

As child and near-corpse games go, it was a real winner.

Back at home for the weekend, I laid claim to the couch for the duration. My husband maintained a safe distance, while still managing to register spousal concern: "You look terrible! Is that cough getting anything up? Like a major organ?"

By Sunday afternoon, I was staring down a nurse practitioner and hoping for either a prescription or referral to a local funeral home. Did I have a cough? Yes. Fever? Yes. Aches and pains? Yes and yes! Did I get a flu shot? Why would I need that?

Then he said those fateful words nobody wants to hear after they have finally convinced themselves that medical intervention is their only hope for a tomorrow.

"It's the flu. There's nothing I can do for you."

He told me to take tea with honey, and aspirin with reckless abandon (not really, but he didn't set any limits, either). He would have prescribed cough syrup with codeine, but Mt. Gummi needs to have her wits about her.

He also said it would last four to five days, and having barely awakened to day four, I'm really hoping five is the charm. Until then I am grateful for the only comforts the flu bug can bring: quality time with the Property Brothers and my Healthy Heart Fair lap robe.

I Hope You Dance

A short while ago, I encouraged readers that when the going gets tough, I hope you dance.

Who knew the Russians read my stuff?

Yeah, they probably don't, but I find it eerily coincidental that dancers from the Mikhailovsky Theatre in St. Petersburg posted an online performance last week that is so hilarious, it's hard to believe they're doing ballet.

Like you and me, the Russian ballet dancers are on partial lockdown due to the coronavirus. Unlike you and me, they are causing viewers to blow their borscht through their noses thanks to their wildly silly spins on a typically classy art form.

It all started when principal dancer Ivan Vasilyev rallied the troupe to produce a three-minute online video for their fans. The

Quarantine Ballet would feature some of Russia's finest, performing everyday household tasks in a balletic kind of way.

Seven Russian dancers threw their tights into the ring, filming themselves performing in the comfort of their own homes, backyards, and one cul-de-sac. I would have to say that professional sports events pale in comparison.

It opens with a ballerina doing high kicks (pas de chat) in her kitchen. She totally nails her upper cupboards. Next up is a male dancer who whirls his bath towel like a matador. Then another ballerina dances around a dropped paring knife while fanning herself with a dinner plate.

Ivan himself gracefully lifts a ballerina toward the stove and back (pas de deux) as she stirs a pot. Then a male ballet dancer prances across his snowy backyard in his shorts with a ballerina perched on his shoulder, and for the grand finale, Ivan leaps and bounds across his street (pas de center line).

It is inspiring and uplifting, and if you try any of it in your own home, you will stretch America's emergency medical resources even thinner. But you will provide personnel with some much-needed comic relief during your reassembly.

The ballet ends with a wild round of canned applause, and each dancer takes an elegant bow or curtsies. The guy with the towel appears with his well-fed pet pug in his arms, which he shifts to graciously accept a spray of plastic flowers.

The dancer performing outside in his shorts bows and then, lacking a stage exit, shrugs and ducks into his children's backyard playhouse. And in the end, two dancers behind an iron gate plaintively reach out to their fans from between the bars, possibly for more plastic flowers.

The Mikhailovsky Theatre recognized its dancers' unorthodox performance with just the kind of sober news release I would expect from my Russian readership:

"Artists remain true to themselves, even in the current unusual conditions. While they do not have the opportunity to interact with spectators at the theatre, the interior of their homes serves as a stage and creative platform for them."

I still hope you dance, but for the sake of our local medical community, please leave the Quarantine Ballet up to the pros.

11. CALL OF THE WILD

Paint Won't Stop Wolf

Staining, staining, on our old shed a-gain!

That's a long "a" in "a-gain," by the way, and do you know the title of the song I stole that line from, then tweaked to suit my shabby needs?

Neither do I. I've been sucking stain fumes all week. What's your excuse?

Pardon me if I sound a bit ill-tempered. In the past two weeks I have stained our shed, our garage, and half our house, then faced down a big bad wolf while armed only with a loaded paintbrush.

I really need to get back to fishing.

The source of my problem is Larry's Ace Hardware in L'Anse. Owner Larry Menard keeps selling me stain, five gallons of California Rustic now, and counting. And do you know what I think? I think Larry could use a little lead in his stain.

I was staining the shed on a warm evening last week when our dog cried wolf. She does it by barking in a higher pitch than usual and running back and forth, close to the house. We've seen her do it a few times now. And we've seen a wolf watch her do it, too.

I looked around and didn't see anything—the wolf's scent must have carried in on the wind—so I went back to my staining. Then all of a sudden a wolf ran out of the woods across the field from the shed, and for the first time ever, our dog was in hot pursuit.

I started hollering after her, because a wolf will turn on a dog and kill it. Then I stopped in mid-holler, because a second wolf came trotting out of the brush between the shed and the woods, and stopped to check my work.

The wolf was less than 30 yards away, and the shed I was staining has no door. I was up on a ladder. If the wolf was a climber, I was kibble. So, taking my cue from a popular fairy tale character he should have been able to relate to, I huffed and I puffed and I let out a roar:

"GET YOUR (insert bad word for wolf's behind) OUTTA' HERE! GIT, WOLF! GIT!"

The wolf didn't move. He didn't even blink. He just stared, then took a couple steps back, then stopped and stared again. To tell the truth, I think he was looking past me to the shed, and I could just see how his evil mind was working:

"California Rustic? What was she thinking? I'd have gone with Terra Cotta."

Irritated by all the noise and obviously disgusted by my color choice, the wolf finally turned and trotted away. Our dog returned safely home shortly after. Only two house walls to go and I'm back on the water again, where the only threatened species are the fish, not the loud lady with the paintbrush.

Whitetail Cafe

Our garden is proof God wants the Michigan deer herd to flourish.

You won't see that one on a church marquee anytime soon. That's because the deer don't need any signs pointing their way to the Whitetail Cafe. We just have to open a seed packet and it calls 'em right in.

It has not always been this way. There was a time when we lived in peace and harmony with nature, planting a garden each spring and, once it sprouted, erecting a mostly ornamental fence around it to gently remind the deer not to eat domestic.

The garden flourished and the deer did, too, politely high-tailing it into the woods whenever they were caught eyeing the produce. When fall came, we would harvest our crop, shoot the deer, and fill the freezer so the circle of Northwoods life would be unbroken.

Then one day a light went on in a big buck's head. He wasn't eating our garden, but we were still going to eat him! He tossed his mighty horns in anger and stomped out to the road, where he was promptly run over by a UPS truck.

But not before the rest of the herd had caught his drift. A vigil was held that night inside our garden fence, refreshments included, and we've been mourning our losses ever since.

At first, the deer waited until late summer to dine at the Whitetail Cafe. They'd come after hours, in the dark of night, chomp a few beets and carrots, and nibble a winter squash for dessert. That was our signal to get the crops in and purchase our hunting licenses.

Then they became even bolder, visiting the produce section mid-summer to get the jump on fellow shoppers. We countered with electric fence: a string of wire that pulsed a dull warning and delivered a sharp shock on contact.

That just attracted the high jumpers and metal heads.

The last straw came last summer when a row of newly sprouted green beans was beheaded in mid-June. Our hunting licenses weren't good until mid-November, so I rolled out our second line of defense, the Wind Chime of Death.

It's a substantial piece of art that usually hangs in our dining room, beyond the reach of both the wind and grandchildren, because it can literally wake the dead. After hanging it from a stout pipe mid-garden, I ran back inside to wait for the deer to hear the music.

Who knew deer loved wind chimes? And dancing too, judging by the fishing line adorned with strips of tinfoil I'd strung over our surviving produce. The deer had tripped on it mid-waltz and dragged it behind them, decapitating whatever was left still standing in our garden.

I mean, "gulag."

Once again I have stretched the limits of responsible word usage tighter than the 10-pound test previously strung between our tomato cages. A gulag is a USSR labor camp. Our vegetable garden just looks like one.

A new six-foot wire fence has been erected around the perimeter of our garden. The garden gate is secured by bungee cords pulled tight enough to strum "Folsom Prison Blues." We wanted to add razor wire and a sentry post, but the garden center was fresh out.

No deer tracks yet! No human ones, either. It's too much work getting into the gulag.

Driving a Death Trap

Of all the cheap journalistic devices I use to snag innocent readers, my favorite would have to be the sensational lead, as in: I am driving a death trap!

If you are still with me, thank you, because degrees don't grow on trees and I paid good money to learn cheap journalistic devices. Also, the lead was 100 percent true because there are currently two mousetraps set inside my car, just waiting for hapless diners to take the bait.

It all started back in 1958 when Mom told Dad, "Of course it's safe, Bob." Nine months later, a baby girl was born who would go far, a little over 400 miles north, to report in a land where nature holds sway and that includes the occasional rodent in your car.

Mice are everywhere in the great Northwoods. They are everywhere in Chicago, too, where I debuted after Mom fibbed to Dad, but there we called them "rats." If they wanted to occupy your car, you didn't argue. You parked it on a side street and took the bus.

Country mice are much less intimidating. Most prefer to live in the wild, but as fall gives way to winter, some yearn for hearth and home, as in the heater of my Subaru Forester.

It happened the fall we decided our garage was a fine place to store a big bag of corn. The mice thought so, too, swiftly moving into the new shopping district and then putting their groceries away under my car hood.

I probably wouldn't have even noticed until that fateful morning when I got into my car, turned the key, and engaged the garbage disposal. Except it wasn't the garbage disposal. It was my heater trying to digest corn.

Then I got shot, from the passenger side heater vent, and the battle was on!

It was only a kernel, but it stung, and rapid bursts of corn fire followed. Then there were more grinding noises as my heater re-loaded, and I was hit with another spray of artillery. So I took my husband's car to work, instead.

A trip to the garage to empty the rodents' pantry cost $100. A trip to the hardware store for traps to catch the shoppers cost about three bucks.

The bag of corn was relocated to a metal garbage can several outbuildings away. We've been smearing peanut butter on little spring-loaded place settings ever since, with plenty of seating available throughout our garage.

This year's trapping season started early. Heavy traffic underfoot had us already setting traps in June. One particularly grisly shift, two customers checked out together, sharing the same fatal bite. It was a banner day, for management at least, at the Rodent Cafe.

Junk recently discovered in my trunk has triggered my new traveling trap line for fall: two traps set right inside my car. I'm really hoping my busy little passenger finds a place setting before my back seat collapses for lack of stuffing, or before his company arrives for the holidays.

From Chicago.

Ursula's Revenge

Awhile back I wrote about a sweet little partridge who'd fallen hard for my husband.

"Veronica" chased his ATV through the woods, and gazed adoringly at him from a stump when he stopped to cut firewood. He even had to move her aside to pile it, and she pecked him once because she thought he was getting a little handsy.

I would like my readers to go on believing those are just the kind of Disney-like woods we live in, minus the animation and music and Zac Efron (I am thinking more Hugh Jackman for my husband's role). But I am a journalist, sworn to objectivity, so I have to tell you about "Ursula," too.

When winter finally gives way to spring, I am compelled to walk through the woods, camera in hand, and take photos of nature in all its splendor. I take the exact same shots every year: ferns uncurling, apple trees blossoming and, for the dark side of nature, a leaf rotting in a water puddle.

You may have seen my work in the newspaper, those little nature shots featured on the top corner of the front page. My most recent contributions were a red bird and a white flower. I guess the dead leaf shot was a bit too edgy.

I was walking down a rutted trail in our woods last week, targeting this year's fern coverage, when I heard something scurrying in the leaves. I stopped in my tracks, trained my lens on the general area for a real, live woodland creature action shot, and out came Ursula.

Like Veronica, Ursula is also a partridge, but there was nothing sweet about her last week. She burst out of the brush with every feather standing at attention, beating her wings furiously against her sides with her beak wide open, hissing at me like a snake.

She came after me at a full run. Because I am the consummate professional, who stands about 5 feet taller and 110 pounds heavier than the bird, I held my ground and snapped three quick photos. Then I turned tail and ran.

Caught in the act, Veronica the partridge shamelessly struts her stuff in front of my bemused husband. Nature can be so cruel.

For the record, if anyone's keeping it, I am not the only one who has been accosted in the woods by a bird gone wild. My friend, John, who stands tall as a tree, looked down one day to see partridge chicks circling his feet and their mama aiming for his throat. John ran, too.

Ursula may have been lower in the pecking order, but she had the upper hand on me, and I beat a retreat to safety. Shortly after, just as my hand had steadied enough to take this year's apple blossom update, there was an even louder crashing in the woods.

This time I'd startled a whitetail deer, maybe the doe who'd been hiding her fawn at the edge of our field, and she retreated with loud, angry huffs. She blew at least a half dozen warnings, probably sending a GPS reading to Ursula, so I ditched the flowers and headed home for the day.

Safe inside again, I settled into my favorite corner of the couch to review this year's spring pictures, and see if Ursula was as photogenic as Veronica had been. That's when I spotted nature's final insult.

A wood tick was crawling up my leg, looking to blend in with my age spots and tuck in for a feast so it could settle down and raise a family of even more ticks to infest our already un-Disney-like woods. I plucked it off and threw it out, hopefully as a tidbit for some passing bird.

Even if it's Ursula.

12. GOING WITH THE TERRITORY

Bad Woman in the Woods

I am a bad woman in the woods.

If this true confession summons visions of a sultry woodland nymph, yeah, hold onto that thought. While you're dreaming, keep an eye out for baddie this deer season in case I have to track a deer beyond our fence line and get hopelessly lost in the neighbor's backyard.

The bad woman reference is actually a nod to the classic documentary "Good Man in the Woods" by Finnish filmmaker Michael Loukinen. Loukinen's film is a shining tribute to the loggers, trappers, and commercial fishermen who carved a life and living out of the wild and rugged U.P.

It is a masterpiece, capturing the stoicism and humility of the woodsmen with some appropriately salty language by the fishermen. I might add that I am a good woman in the boat, mostly because the sides are high enough to keep me from tipping into the drink. Also, because I know the lingo and am not afraid to use it.

But this is not a confessional about tipsiness and cussing. It is a confessional about having a character shaped by inner-city living my first 21 years and Northwoods bumbling for the next 40, and counting.

I'm right "UP" there with the guys in Loukinen's movie! I just process it all a little differently.

For instance, I know firsthand why Queen Elizabeth always walks ahead of Prince Philip. It's so he doesn't whack her backwards with a tree limb because she's following him too closely through the woods on one of their royal hunts.

As a bad woman in the woods, I too have felt the sting because I choose to follow. I follow because my husband knows where the heck we are, and is often holding a loaded bird gun while we get wherever we are going.

After so many years of picking brush out of my teeth, you would think I'd allow for some clearance, but that is not the stuff of a bad woman in the woods. Getting brush-whacked every fall is a rite of passage. It is also nature's own exfoliator.

Then there is the matter of direction. On a walk through the deep dark woods just last week, I told my husband if anything ever happened to him I'd never get out alive. He took five steps out to our pickup (where did that come from?) and said I'd eventually come out on a road.

It's a scientific fact, put forth by an actual scientist, that most people's legs are different lengths. You can't even tell until the day you're hopelessly lost in the woods and running tight circles around a tree, even though the road and pickup are probably just five short steps away.

Finally, there is the problem of the landscape. It's all woods out there. On a recent hike I asked my husband how he knew exactly where we were. He looked out across the woods and said, "We're right by them oaks, and that swamp is down there."

I looked across the woods and saw a bunch of trees. Then I looked at that swamp down there and saw a bunch more trees. And both bunches of trees looked pretty much the same to me because, let's face it, they're trees.

A good woman in the woods would have nodded knowingly and led the way back to the pickup, naturally compensating for her scientifically shorter leg. I nodded unknowingly and fell into step behind him, a little close but just right for a bad woman in the woods.

Master Canner

Please select the correct ending to the following sentence:
You know it's spring in the U.P. when--

A. The crocuses are up!

B. The robins return!

C. The beer cans bloom in the ditches.

If your answer was C, we obviously share the same entrepreneurial spirit. Also, don't bother with my road because the Master Canner was already out pedaling for profit this past weekend, earning her fortune one dime at a time.

Thanks to its 10 cent deposit on cans and bottles, Michigan is a land where beverages are always overpriced. Also, a land of opportunity where anyone with a plastic bag and a strong gag reflex can get paid for picking litter.

Spring is prime time for pickers because tossers have had a full season of disposing of their cans and bottles in a highly illegal manner. And because the winter season spans approximately half the U.P. calendar year, the pickin's ain't slim.

Most of the cans deposited on roadsides are from the beer family. That is because they cost so much more than the 10 cent deposit when an officer of the law discovers one or twelve in your vehicle. Pop drinkers also litter, but only when their snoose can is full.

The annual spring melt unearths a regular treasure trove of returnable cans and bottles. It also unearths a lot of earth in the form of mud, and water in the form of former snow. It's just like the popular reality show "Gold Rush," minus the gold and swearing.

Some swearing may occur, but only when you step in deep water to pick a can and find out it's from Wisconsin (no deposit, no return). Picker courtesy dictates you keep the can anyway, but sometimes you are swearing too loudly to listen.

By now you are probably wondering how a mere picker can claim the title "Master Canner." Well, first you have to make sure nobody edits your work before you get it into print. Then you have to pursue your craft with dogged determination, starting as a mere slip of a picker.

I remember it like it was 50-some years ago, because yesterday is already kind of a blur. Feeling the need for an ice cream cone from Tastee-Freeze, my little inner city friends and I would go and ask Mrs. Gorb if we could return her pop bottles for the two cent deposits.

She was elderly and kind and probably didn't even drink pop, but her tenants did and they stored their bottles under her apartment building staircase. We'd dig them out, tip them upside down in the alley and shake out the dead water bugs before heading for the store.

Except they weren't actually water bugs. They were la cucarachas.

I think you can tell what a la cucaracha is. And I think you know by now why it doesn't bother me a bit, even in farm country, to pick cans out of ditches for fun and profit in the spring. I'm not just picking bouquets of beer cans. I am cleaning up the earth.

As long as there's no snoose involved.

New Car Blues

Have you ever dropped an easy pop-up and lost the ballgame?

Earned a dishonorable mention in your local newspaper's District Court News?

The same week your mom bought a subscription?

Don't tell me about shame! I am driving a brand new vehicle in the U.P.

I am sure there are civilizations that celebrate new possessions. I think they are in Los Angeles, CA. In the Upper Peninsula, MI, quite the opposite is true. What was good enough for our ancestors is good enough for us. We know, because we're still using it.

The fractious hay baler that outlived them will be the death of us yet. We've learned to duck from the splitting maul that flies off the handle. And those rust spots in the bottom of the baby bathtub in the sauna? They provide grip to help keep baby above the water line.

We live in a cyclic region, and we are a recyclic people. After an appliance has breathed its last, we will shock it back into service for another decade or so with the most important tool in every Finlander's war chest. It's called sisu.

Sisu is the pride that will not permit you to throw anything away, no matter how many years of hard time it's already served. When the fender broke off our ATV, it was stitched back on with wire and sisu. Ditto for our ice fishing scoop, only thinner wire and a little less sisu.

I inherited a warped electric skillet that my dad, a food broker, had used in store demos over 40 years ago. When a leg broke off, the skillet disappeared into our basement. A few days later, it rose again, sporting a new leg carved from a piece of deer antler. Extreme sisu.

Sometimes even extreme sisu is not enough to keep a contraption alive, like our aged Toyota with over 200,000 miles on its belts. Maybe it was the oil leak. Or the rusting brake lines. Or the little strips of electric tape peeling off the warning lights on my dashboard.

Against all that my husband/mechanic stands for, we left home in the dark of one night, crossed the state line, and slipped back in the next day with a brand new vehicle. The make and color are being withheld to protect the guilty. Don't worry, we catch it plenty on the local level.

"Someone's got money!"

"Mind if I test drive that out on the Plains?"

"It's not nearly as ugly as your old car was."

And so on and so forth until I am truly regretting not purchasing the heavily tinted window package.

A pre-owned car comes complete with scratches, stains, dents, and stray condiment packets. A new car is just a clean slate in need of a reality check. Ours is slowly earning its stripes, both inside and out.

Three thousand miles into the warranty, I have recently resumed transporting small children with a minimum of fuss. Mine, not theirs. I'm back to throwing my fishing rod in the trunk (bait still attached comes at 5,000 miles or more), and just last week, I gave a needy hound dog a ride home.

I was driving to town when I saw the dog on the highway, looking balefully at cars as they slowed down to navigate around him. He was soaked from running through tall, dewy grass, and was trailing a broken lead. When I stopped and gave a whistle, he happily galloped over to my car.

His tag pegged him as a local, so I opened my hatchback and he got halfway in. His second half needed a lift. Once inside, he did what all wet, dirty dogs do in the light cream interior of a new car. He shook himself off, really hard.

I wiped the dirt out of my eyes and beat it for his home. When he started to pace in the back, I prayed the prayer of new car owners everywhere who pick up wet strays: "Please don't let that big dirty hound dog jump all over my new car. Amen."

In answer to my prayers, he didn't jump. Instead, he tipped his head back and mourned the fact he was riding in a new sedan instead of a rusty, battered, respectable pickup held together by plenty of sisu.

"BaROOOOO!" said the big dirty hound dog. "BaROOOOOOOOOOO!"

We made it to his home in record time, and my car cleaned up just fine. I am ashamed to admit I actually vacuumed, but it is a free country after all, full of friendly dogs and free ranging deer and sticky-fingered grandchildren in need of transportation.

I'll be holding my head high again real soon.

After a little convincing, the old Ford 8N tractor we use for mowing begins its faithful rounds, making hay while the sun shines.

We Make Hay

Sung to the tune of "Dixieland":

Away up north in the land of Watton
It's too cold for growin' cotton
We make hay, we make hay
We make hay, we make hay

If you think "we make hay" alludes to romance, you are struggling under a serious misconception. Better you should struggle under a nice hefty hay bale. Make that several hundred. Be sure to visit soon!

Who am I kidding? Nobody visits us in July. It is the month of haymaking, when days run long, tempers run short, and tractors run only after a tug down the driveway, and sometimes a couple of laps around the field.

Hay is what happens when people don't mow their lawns until July. I learned about hay later in life because my people were urban. They pulled their agricultural roots generations ago, trading tractor keys for bus tokens to pursue fulfilling lives in the city. Mostly, waiting in traffic.

We didn't cut grass because it only occurred between cracks in the sidewalk. In wide open spaces, called suburbs, people passed ordinances requiring regular mowing to prevent unsightly infestations of haymaking equipment.

All of this was lost on me years ago when I came north, presumably to work and fish, and was bedazzled by a countryman. As we stood at the edge of his field, I blinked back tears at the beauty of all that grass waving in the wind, sneezed, and said, "I do!"

We've been making hay every summer since. It still brings a tear to my eye. And sweat to my brow, scratches to my arms, and words to my lips that my people used to reserve for heavy traffic.

We mow it down, rake two days later
Pray our geriatric baler
Doesn't quit,' fore we git,
All our hay, squared away

The problem with haymaking is, we're small potatoes so we annually get whipped. For two weeks of the year, we revive ancient farm implements stored on Cemetery Road (for good reason) to cough, wheeze, and snort across seven fields of green.

And the equipment doesn't sound much better.

We pick the bales up by hand and haul them with pickup trucks to the barn, where they're stacked to the ceiling. We do it on the hottest days of the year. We need to lay some major pavement around here.

Ha ha! I am such a kidder! It is how I survive haymaking. And I had better come up with fresh material soon because we have a whole new generation of haymakers coming up the ranks. They are called "grandchildren."

They rode in the pickup for the first time last year, one-year-old Dawson in his car seat already admiring the tractors, and his sister, three-year-old Maddy, bouncing happily along with a juice box in hand until she fell asleep across my lap. Two more little hayseeds had been planted.

This year we recruited two mossier hands, their dad, Matt, and our friend, Mack, Professor of English Emeritus at Kent State University. Mack's credits were a little dodgy, but he did a fine job piloting the pickup with the grandchildren on board. He didn't even dent the barn.

After a rain delay we'll finish the job this week, then pack it all up for another year of rest until July rolls around again. That gives me 11 months to heal, to forget, and to work on that ordinance requiring frequent lawn mowing in Watton.

Oh I'm glad I live in Watton,
Hooray! Hooray!
In Watton, Mich., we hunt and fish,
And like to plant large gardens and
Make hay, make hay, make hay up
Noooooooooorth, in Watton!

13. PAST? PERFECT!

Poly Preserves History

With dripping paintbrush in hand, I paused at the precipice. Do I erase history, or do I preserve it? And then I struck.

The brush was fully loaded with polyurethane varnish in my favorite flavor, high gloss. The history was evident on our not-so-gently used dining room floor. Thanks to my deep and abiding respect for the past, its past is a whole lot shinier now.

Who am I kidding? Surely not family and friends who have come to know me for what I truly am: a bum who is too lazy to remove scratches, dents, and other crimes against wood before hitting it with a fresh coat of poly.

There are two driving forces in my dedication to slopping shiny varnish on all things wood and slightly battered. The first is my alma mater, Francis M. McKay elementary school in Chicago, IL. The school was built back in 1928, and it kind of showed.

The floors were hardwood; the desks still had inkwells; and long poles with brass attachments were used to open tall windows from the top. School smelled like varnish every September, thanks to the fresh coat the janitors had slapped onto every dulled surface over the summer.

We had two janitors at McKay, Ed and Herman. Neither had the time nor inclination to refinish miles of hardwood flooring and wooden desk tops before the students returned in the fall. Opting for quantity over quality--why sand away good wood with bad?-- they let the polyurethane flow.

Scratches on floors and childhood sweethearts' names carved into desktops reappeared in the fall, shinier than ever. We students took pride in our gleaming halls of learning, and in the loud squeaks of our back-to-school sneakers on freshly varnished, well-trod hardwood.

The second driving force in my addiction to keeping the past presentable is *Antiques Roadshow*. The public TV series invites people to bring their old treasures in to be appraised by the pros. For instance, according to the appraisers, ugly old paintings are worth gazillions.

That is not entirely true. They like ugly modern paintings, too. Hang onto all your paintings. Even more important, don't refinish old stuff to make it look new again, or you will erase its value and be embarrassed to death when you appear on *Antiques Roadshow*.

The pros love "patina." It's the film on weathered metal and the dull sheen on old furniture. Our ancestors worked their fingers to the bone removing patina, and our future fortunes along with it. Thank them, if you get the chance. Then run for your life.

My approach to preserving the past is a fine blend of both influences. I truly appreciate the history behind our priceless possessions. I just want my old stuff to last longer and look a little shinier.

The blanket chest my husband's dad and brother crafted for our wedding gift became a toy box for our children. Our son used his toy wooden hammer to add some patina to its lid. At the time, I wanted to add some patina to his head.

Franklin was a cat of extra toes, and many claws. He loved to lie on the wooden mantel between the living and dining rooms so he could watch TV while monitoring his food dish. When he heard the kibble hit the bowl, he scrambled for purchase on the slippery shelf, then dove.

I didn't discipline Franklin, either, because he was more heavily armed than me. But I remember him fondly, and our little carpenter too, every time I add another layer of shine to our well-preserved family history.

Valuables Safe from Us

My friend Martha Bloomfield once wrote a fan letter to Pete Seeger and got a postcard from him in return. She put it in a safe place and hasn't seen it since.

The moral of the story is, I am not afraid to do some major name dropping to reel in my readers. Martha once headlined in a feature in our local weekly newspaper! Pete was a pretty darn good singer in his own right, too.

But this story is not about morals. It is about safe places. The only thing they're safe from is us.

Throughout our lives, there are all manner of things we want to keep safe from others. First it's our candy from our siblings. Then it's our diaries. Next comes money and important papers until we come full circle and are back to hiding our candy again, this time from my husband.

I mean, "our spouses." Thanks to man's inventiveness, we have safes to keep our things safe. They include bank safes and gun safes and those cute little house safes with a handle for your robber's convenience. Also, safe deposit boxes and locking file cabinets.

Thanks to man's squirreliness, we tuck our valuables instead into the darnedest of places, until we can get to the bank and our safe deposit box. Or until we can remember where we put our cute little house safe, unless the robber has already walked off with it.

It's not like we don't have a system. The house safe keys go in the gravy boat in the china cabinet. They're guaranteed to surface on holidays, and the gravy helps keep the lock working smoothly.

Important papers go in the desk because the file cabinet is so full of canceled checks and appliance manuals, it tips forward when you open its drawers. Desk drawers are designated because grandchildren also use them for art supplies, and the IRS frowns on colored statements.

Coins just slightly older than us are stored in a coffee can. Some folks bury their coin collections, never to be seen again. Ours sits in front of the file cabinet to prevent tipping when an appliance is acting up.

All of the above are your basic no-brainer safe places for the things we treasure most, or might get called out on by the IRS. It is when we try to find a safe place for items that are over the top, like a postcard from a pretty darn good singer, that we go off the radar.

Here is to just a few of the things I've saved and never seen again. They include, in order of disappearance: Mama Bear, Jane West's hitching post, an empty pocket watch case, my St. Christopher medal, and a blue toddler's spring jacket with ribbon accents.

I strongly suspect my mother was responsible for redistributing most of the above, except for my daughter's jacket, which I'm pretty sure I left in a cart at K-Mart. But I'm proud to state that I cracked a safe place just last week when I solved the Case of the Missing Passports.

I distinctly remembered removing them from our glove box after our trip to Canada and assuring my husband, "I'll put them in a safe place." It was so safe, I spent a tense day searching for where I'd cleverly secured them, finally finding them tucked into his underwear drawer.

In case we ever go Down Under.

Confessions of a Collector

A few weeks ago, I was invited to display my collection of old fishing lures at a library open house.

What collection of old fishing lures?

My dented tackle box is chock-full with a dynamic assortment of gluey rubber worms, spinners without skirts, and Grandpa's rusted jig with rooster feathers. All are still in use, thank you very much, so I offered up my nesting doll collection instead.

It includes three old nesting dolls. One is incomplete due to innards gone AWOL. Two are exactly the same, and the paint on all three is chipped from being dropped by grandchildren. Regrettably, the library's collection quota had just been filled. Check with us next time!

Collecting is an art form, and I am clearly an artist. My first collection was Many Stuffed Animals. I slept with them, took them for buggy rides, and packed them into my Davy Crockett suitcase every time I ran away from home, even though I wasn't allowed to cross the street.

With three older brothers constantly egging me on, we circled our block pretty often.

Next came Art Projects I Would Never Finish. Tastefully displayed on a dusty shelf in the dining room closet, it included several paint by numbers kits, my Touch 'N Tuck picture of a palomino's head, a candle kit just like Theresa Banky's, and all things related to sewing.

Mom eventually redistributed that collection to children who had an ounce of perseverance. I moved on, moved out, and got an apartment in the U.P. which soon housed my new collection of Stuff People Can't Fit in Their Own Homes—Hey, Doesn't Nancy Have a New Unfurnished Apartment?

Before I knew it, I was dining at Mrs. Magnuson's kitchen table, watching Grandma Emerson's black and white TV set with rabbit ears included, and walking wide circles around co-worker Tom Caylor's couch of ill repute.

Then I married, and the time came to move my collection to the country. The kitchen table regrettably went back across the street; the couch regrettably survived the trip; and the TV came to rest in the basement where the children would someday watch cartoons "the old-fashioned way."

Did I say "basement?" Pardon my faux pas, because our lower level is obviously an exhibition area for the family's finest collection to date. Its title is simple, yet elegant: Scraps of Wood We'll Use Later.

Scraps of Wood We'll Use Later was started when we built our home. Whether we were cutting a few inches off a wall stud, a couple feet off a trim board, or splitting a shim so the couch wouldn't wobble, my husband would invariably say, "Save that scrap. We'll use it later."

At the end of a long summer, we had a strong start on a lovely new log home, and a scrap pile that blocked the sun. There were log ends and warped boards, jagged pieces of siding, and a broken hammer handle. It was a veritable treasure trove for a woman who'd once refused to melt wax.

I have whittled away at that pile for 30 years now, looking over my shoulder every time I tuck another stray piece of scrap into the wood stove. I mourn art projects that might have been, but take comfort in both a slowly dwindling collection and a promise well kept because we heat with wood: we're using it later.

Ugly Couch Finds Fame

Our couch is famous!

Don't come over to see it just yet, please, because we're still roping off the viewing area with binder twine. We're also positioning our reading lamps just so, to bring out the best in a sofa that recently starred on the wildly popular daytime TV show "Regis and Kelly."

It all started when Walmart was clearing out tomato plants for only 25 cents each. We had already committed to putting in only six plants this summer, since last year's crop rivaled that of Italy, but reverting to type we somehow wound up with 14.

Most tomatoes don't ripen in U.P. gardens. They ripen in U.P. basements, spread out on cardboard on the floor. By early September, we have to travel hand-over-hand across the clothesline to get to the freezer. To fire the stove, we throw in three sticks of wood and two tomatoes.

The tomatoes carpeting our basement typically refuse to ripen until the weather turns beautiful, or a friend calls to make a shopping date. Then a bushel and a half spontaneously blush and require my immediate attention.

On a sunshiny morning a few weeks back, I filled two pressure canners with quarts of tomato juice and felt my way through the steam to the living room. Flopping down onto the couch, I switched on the TV and heard Kelly Ripa say those three words that would secure our sofa's future fame: "Ugly Couch Contest."

I'd missed most of the lead-in, but the gist of it was that Regis and Kelly were sponsoring an ugly couch contest, and the three finalists were in. And in the very next frame, there sat the twin to the couch I was sitting on, vying for the ugliest on daytime TV.

I sat mesmerized as its unfortunate owner (I'll bet she has tomatoes in her basement, too) talked about her couch. She said it was about 30 years old, practically an antique, and hid stains well. Regis gave her a sympathetic pat on the arm and went on to the next aberration of furniture.

Personally, I think she sold it a bit short. If it had been me, I'd have spread my hankie on the cushion beside me and sat Reeg down for a proper visit. After the dust had settled, I'd tell him the full story of how the ugly old couch came to be ours.

About 10 years ago, we were shopping for a brand new couch. I had narrowed the field to a cute little number in heather blue when my husband came home from the co-op and announced there was an even better deal on the bulletin board.

The ad was for a couch AND chair, both in brown plaid, for a mere $150. I had my reservations, but was young and gullible and terminally cheap, so we gathered up the kids, fired up the pickup and set out to keep our date with destiny.

The elderly couple who were selling it had dimmed the lights a bit before we arrived, but the sight still took our breath away. It wasn't exactly plaid. It was more of a patchwork quilt design, and every patch was homelier than its neighbor.

The man loved his old couch. His wife noted the side he always sat on was even more worn than the other. But she had her heart set on a new one, probably something in heather blue. So it had to go, preferably without him still on it.

I thought the couch was uglier than original sin, but I didn't have the heart to say it in front of the obviously grieving man. Instead, we marveled at its fine lines and considerable size, stopping short of noting you could drop a Thanksgiving dinner on it and not detect a stain, and sealed the deal.

Both couch and chair fit in surprisingly well, and have been faithful servants since. Babies burp on them, guests sink into them, and they keep coming back for more. The furniture, that is. They've stood the test of time with only a few new rips and sags since that dear old man left his mark.

By this time, Regis would have been using my hankie to wipe away his tears, after shaking the dust off it first. Unfortunately I missed the contest deadline, and could only watch as my sofa's twin lost the title to a custom-made monstrosity.

The winner got money. Runners-up got slipcovers. I got back to my tomatoes.

Trail of Broken Toys

When I was a kid, my toys were worth millions.

I had it all: a little magenta-haired troll in a sailor suit, a Betsy Wetsy doll in something waterproof, Jane West and her palomino, Flame, and a real live Kenner Easy Bake Oven complete with cake and cookie mixes.

And just like a kid, I played it all away.

That's because collectively, the toys were worth about 50 bucks tops, or less if Betsy wet them. They might have been worth a small fortune today if I'd only had the foresight to store them all away, in original packaging, and break my brothers' stuff instead.

I see it all the time on my laptop, when I should be spending my time in a more productive manner but baking with light bulbs has left me slightly dim. Besides, scrolling can be very soothing—until a pop-up suddenly declares one of your former toys is now worth a king's ransom.

Just yesterday, I was conducting important research on Facebook when my computer informed me a 1954 Superman lunch box had recently sold for over $13,000.

I distinctly remember carrying a metal lunch box to school, with a thermos inside held in place by metal brackets. The box always smelled like peanut butter on white bread and the milk was always lukewarm. I don't remember what was on the lid.

Knowing my penchant for all things Western, it was probably *The Rifleman*, now worth a cool $200. Recalling my brothers' penchant for pushing their kid sister into bushes on the way to school, today it would be scratched, dented, and worthless.

And it would still smell like peanut butter on white bread and lukewarm milk.

Back to scrolling for dollars, I just looked up my Kenner Easy-Bake Oven and it's going for $120 on eBay. Unfortunately it's also long gone, a victim of too many cakes that took too long to bake when I had other fish to fry, like playing kick-the-can with my friends in the alley.

The brothers could be rolling in it too today, if they'd just taken a little better care of G.I. Joe and his green Foot Locker ($250), their Lionel train set (king's ransom), and even their Boy Scout handbooks (hardcover, 1960, $330).

Instead, we left behind a trail of destruction on our march to adulthood, squandering future fortunes like so many beheaded Barbies and dog-eared Archie comic books. Except for the few rare, not-for-profit exceptions.

I treasure toys that barely survived my childhood. That's cowgirl Jane West's whip at center, in pristine condition because Flame was always a good horse.

When the grandchildren get bored, I invite them to join me before a small bureau in the spare bedroom. We sit on the floor together, and I reverently open its drawers to bask in the glow of the treasures it holds; like Indiana Jones in the Ark of the Covenant, minus the disturbing Nazis.

It's full of stuff I just can't let go of, like Betsy's well-worn clothespins, a stuffed squirrel Mom bought me at a gas station on her way to drop me off at college, a tiny china teapot from the set I bought with my own money in grade school, and even my kindergarten diploma.

It's just a bunch of junk. I wouldn't sell it for a million bucks.

14. BAD HOUSEKEEPING

Stencil Artist Crosses Borders

It lurked in darkness for time immemorial. It knew not hunger, no want nor need, until that fateful day when a trembling hand reached in, closed around it, and the madness was unleashed.

I'm stenciling again!

For those who are not schooled in the fine arts, stenciling is for people who can't even paint by numbers. You take a plastic sheet with designs punched out, tape it to a wall, brush paint over the holes, and as we say in the U.P., Viola! There's English Ivy all over your house.

Stenciling was huge back in the 1980s, and there were patterns for every room in the house. You had your Nouveau Rose in the dining room, Bouncing Bunnies circling the nursery, and Ducks in the Marsh bordering the room that boasted the most head mounts.

Stenciling usually occurred high on the wall so the kids couldn't smear it while it was drying. Best of all, you could slop it on, I mean, "execute your artwork," between laundry loads or during Mister Rogers' Neighborhood.

If I may say so myself, because nobody else will, I was a master of my craft. I stenciled borders. Then closet doors. Then headboards, dressers, and chairs. Then I capped my paints and buried my stencils on a high closet shelf because I clearly had a problem with fine art.

Years passed, and my Morning Glories in the bathroom and Autumn Splendor in our son's bedroom went with them. If you look hard, you can still spot traces of The Vineyard in the hallway, kind of like the Mona Lisa peering through the mist.

Then my daughter brought the madness back to light.

It started innocently enough, with gifts my sister-in-law, Gail, had made when our children were born. She burned their vital stats onto wooden plaques and varnished them to a high sheen, lest we ever forget I brought three 8-plus pound babies into the world.

That's my take on it, anyway. Our youngest, now a mom of two, also wants to lord her babies' birth weights over them in the future, because she asked me to do what Gail did, minus the obvious woodworking talent.

How hard could it be? I burn wood all the time! As a matter of fact, detecting a chill, I just threw another log in.

First I acquired a burn permit, just to be on the safe side. Then I bought stencils so my letters and numbers would be uniform. Then I burned them into plaques my husband made. Then I noticed I had a lot of empty wood still showing around the edges.

So I just decided to fill in the spaces.

My husband leaped up when he heard the scratch of the kitchen chair by the back bedroom closet (he never fully appreciated all those vines and acorns stenciled overhead), but the tools were already in my steely grip. It was time for me to make my mark on the next generation.

I was thinking Spring Bouquet.

The little tubes of latex paint with dippy names brought back a flood of happy memories. Like the masters before me, I based my color selections on what hadn't dried up, and got busy filling in the holes. In no time flat I had those plaques popping in hues of Lilac Dust and Carolina Blue.

"Honey!" I called, my fully loaded stenciling brush still in hand, taking in our home's white open spaces with my artist's eye. "You need to find me a new hiding place!"

Substitute Chef

I cannot overemphasize the importance of following recipes to the letter.

I can't, because I don't.

I am the Substitute Chef. I substitute white flour for wheat, canola for corn oil, rice for noodles, and skip cilantro altogether because to me, it tastes like soap. I also thicken with cornstarch instead of flour, and treat all beans as if they were created equal.

Skim milk pinch hits for whole, and dark chocolate makes any recipe better, especially ones calling for white chocolate which isn't really chocolate. Canned tomatoes step in for stewed, and broth is just another word for bouillon cubes.

If any of the above is starting to make you hungry, you are not a member of either my family or social circle. Let's do lunch sometime! Your place, not mine.

Before you start cooking, I might also add that my taste for substitution runs a little on the wild side. Literally. I freely substitute wild game for nice, fat, juicy barnyard animals that never had to run/swim/fly for their lives from Nancy.

Trust me, it makes a difference.

If a recipe calls for chicken, I will liberate a partridge from our freezer. If my spaghetti or chili or meat loaf recipes call for hamburger, I substitute venison, venison, or venison. And no bones about it, my pickled northern pike beats store-bought pickled herring every time.

Pickled pike is one of the pitiful few triumphs that emerge from my substitute kitchen. Admittedly, the venison burger has been known to pass muster too, but sending in a partridge for a fatted hen is a culinary crime, especially when it's served slightly leaded.

My reasons for not following the written word are equal parts geography and lifestyle, except for dark chocolate which is a no-brainer. As a proud Upper Michigander, I live miles from the nearest grocery store. When I finally arrive at the store, I prefer to shop on the cheap.

My shopping cart brakes at orange tags in dairy, where dated jalapeno cheese will add just the right zip to my lasagna. It will also complement that venison hamburger impersonating Italian sausage: add garlic powder & oregano, and there you go! Guaranteed leftovers.

My cart also stops for generics, another great addition to a gamey cook's arsenal. Cream of mushroom soup can be used to doctor a wide range of tasty dishes, from partridge casserole to ground venison casserole to venison lasagna if you're fresh out of generic spaghetti sauce.

Many of the above figured into last night's menu, which was my Northwoods take on celebrity chef Gordon Ramsay's delicious Quick Chicken and Rice Noodle Stir Fry. Care to take a stab at my substitutions?

I couldn't find rice noodles at the store, so I used white rice instead. We don't have a wok, so I non-stuck with Teflon. Who needs sesame oil when you have canola? And thanks to a bountiful hunting season, two partridges were able to fly the frozen coop to step in for the chicken.

Leftovers, anyone?

The Truffles I've Seen

My truffles began when my husband suggested we celebrate our 20th wedding anniversary with a motorcycle tour of the Keweenaw Peninsula

This would not be a bad idea, if only he'd had the foresight to marry Cher. Cher would toss back her luscious mane, adjust her leather halter top, snuggle up behind him and whisper, "I got you, babe!"

Instead, he married one of the Andrews sisters.

"Are you crazy?" I asked, "or am I just over-insured?"

For a date's sake, I finally relented, and a good thing it was because I learned some valuable lessons on the back of that Honda Goldwing. First of all, we live 18 Hail Mary's from our neighboring town of Covington. Second, I now know the secret to successful candy making.

Once we hit Covington, I opened my eyes, quit praying, and enjoyed the rest of the ride. An underlying level of tension lingered, though, surfacing whenever the helmet in front of my face turned left or right and sometimes, I swear, 180 degrees to enjoy the scenery.

"WATCH THE ROAD!" I'd bellow into the wind stream, followed by a whap on my husband's helmet. The bike would twitch, he'd mumble (not a prayer), then the helmet would once again center itself between my beloved's knotted shoulders.

This went on for, oh, most of the ride until we ran out of road at the tip of the peninsula and had to turn back towards home. Soon after navigating Brockway Mountain Drive, a steep and scenic pass liberally dotted with helmet whaps, my driver turned into the Jampot to clear his head.

The Jampot is a tiny store run by monks who have dedicated their lives to making mankind even more well-rounded. They do this by selling tons of delicious home baked goods, jams, jellies, and more during the no-snow season. And there isn't a label or price tag in the shop.

The day we strode in, there were approximately 20 tourists stuffed into the tiny store and one beleaguered monk at the register. Upon finally reaching the front of the line, each and every customer would ask, "Whatcha' got?", and the monk would sigh deeply and repeat the litany.

"Thimbleberry jam, raspberry jam, cranberry muffins, chocolate chip muffins, fruitcake, oatmeal cookies," and on and on, fulfilling some vow he must have taken that will pay off big time in the afterlife. Then the next customer would belly up to the counter, smile and ask, "Whatcha' got?"

By the time we reached the counter, my husband's headache was almost gone. We spared the monk and cut to the chase, ordering a raisin bran cupcake and an item that appealed to my personal sense of adventure, a frosted rum raisin brownie.

We sat down on the stoop outside, and faced with the healthy choice or hard liquor, I nabbed the brownie. My driver had to stay sober so I only shared a little, and in a surprisingly short time I decided I really liked motorcycling in the Keweenaw, and everywhere else, too!

After securing me behind him with two bungee cords, my husband enjoyed a blissfully uninterrupted return trip. Back home and with my head finally cleared, I decided I was going to start baking with hard liquor.

I do not have a good reputation for baking. I blame the constant shrilling of our fire alarm overhead. But if a rum raisin brownie could bring me comfort on the back of a big, bad motorcycle, then a dab of spirits could surely make my homemade Christmas candies sing.

I set about collecting recipes that were 80 proof and up, and by the time Christmas came, I'd narrowed the field to three clear winners: bourbon balls, brandied cherries, and chocolate truffles. Next came a trip to the co-op for that necessary ingredient, a wee pint of cheer.

I studied the liquor section for the best (cheapest) bottle of spirits to be found. I engaged the assistance of a friendly cashier. Then a helpful customer joined in, then a neighbor, and before you knew it, everyone in the store was helping Nancy shop for booze.

"Here's bourbon. No, forget that. It's over $10 a pint."

"Here's a bottle, only $3.50!"

"That's blackberry brandy. She wants to make candy, not cure irregularity."

It was a touching Christmas scene, if a little unsettling, and in the end we all agreed that Kessler Whiskey at a sensible $2.50 a pint was just what my recipes needed. Clutching my treasure in an appropriate brown paper bag, I headed home to bake some Christmas magic.

The bourbon (Kessler Whiskey) balls were a hit. A relative popped one into her mouth and proclaimed, "I like the bourbon balls." Three later, she said, "I REALLY like the bourbon balls!" Then we introduced her to strong coffee and Russian Tea Cakes.

The brandied (again, Kessler Whiskey) cherries were even more sodden. Who knew cherries had a problem with alcohol? The recipe called for an overnight soak of maraschino cherries in brandy, then a quick dip in melted chocolate and back in the fridge to set. They set well with our guests, too.

The truffles proved my only disappointment. With only two tablespoons of booze per recipe, they were rather sobering, and slumped dejectedly in their candy cups. I'll give both them and us a lift next year with a hearty dose of, you guessed it, leftover Kessler Whiskey!

I've already applied for a liquor license for next year's Christmas candy making. I'm also working on a label, illustrated of course with your favorite back seat rider, a plateful of treats in one hand and the other hovering over her driver's helmet with the warning:

"Don't eat and drive, and remember to fasten your bungee cords."

Bridal Shower Revisited

I was eating cereal from a plastic bowl with bunnies on it and drinking coffee from our chipped Air Force One cup when I had a revelation.

After 27 years of marriage, I could use me another bridal shower.

I know that last sentence was grammatically suspect, but I've got bigger fish to fry, in my electric pan that has a potbelly and three legs. My stock has taken a beating over time. Before I go to my final reward, I'd like just one last meal on a matched set of dishes that don't feature Scooby Doo smiling back at me.

Bridal showers, like endless summer days and joints that bend without complaint, are wasted on the young. Kids can live on love. People who have blown out the candles on their 25th wedding anniversary cake, two tries minimum, deserve a bath towel that didn't belong to Holiday Inn first.

The formula is set in stone. We start out with next to nothing, and wind up about the same way. In between there is a period of great bounty thanks to the modern tradition of arming the bride-to-be, turning her loose in a major department store, and encouraging her to shoot.

She isn't aiming for a headline on CNN. She is using a bar code scanner to select gifts for her bridal shower registry.

Dishes that match, cutlery with perfect posture, sheets and pillow cases you can hang outside and still hold your head high! So young and innocent, yet with an aim like Jesse James. It brings a tear to this former's bride's eye, like trying to read a menu without my magnifiers.

I too was once a blushing bride-to-be, but we didn't pack bar code scanners back then. We had helpful hints we freely dropped, which were patently ignored by brides who had already stood the test of time, and now knew better.

"She wants fancy-schmancy plates? You know how those things chip! The girl gets Corelle Ware, autumn pattern for a fall wedding."

"Crystal wine glasses? He works construction. Who they gonna' entertain? A nice, lidded cake pan can travel to church for coffee and bring better stuff back home. I'll throw in a recipe or two."

"Canning jars. They got a garden, they'll need canning jars. Tupperware you get when the margarine's gone."

And so on and so forth until our kitchen and home were fully equipped for our married life in the U.P. I loved my Corelle, and still have a piece or two. I'm on my third cake pan, minus its lid. Through the years I've acquired a lifetime supply of canning jars and margarine cups.

And yet, I want the scanner.

Top off that drink, the one you're sipping from a Flintstones jelly jar, and try to tell me you don't have an itchy trigger finger, too. Twenty-five years was silver, but if I was smart, I'd have gone for the gold: a second bridal shower for the next quarter century.

I'd do it all so differently this time around. I wouldn't drop hints. I'd wield my scanner with a vengeance. I'd spray the store with a volley of gift registry scans that would have fellow shoppers running for cover, and my shower guests digging deeper into their purses.

There would be no stopping a bride of 27 years who's been showering for the past five behind a plastic curtain that should be labeled HAZMAT. I'd have my fancy schmancy plates, and I'd eat off them, too, right after knocking down a new lid in Housewares for my topless cake pan.

I'd target cookware that's never doubled as a drum set for a toddler. Bed & Bath would take a hit, though bathroom scales would obviously dodge the bullet. In Small Appliances, I'd wing an electric fry pan that still had both its figure and four good legs.

When the air finally cleared, the carnage would be great, but I'd have one scan left, saved for Sporting Goods. New His & Hers Blue Enamel coffee mugs would be just the thing to toast the old bride and groom's happy future. And they're guaranteed not to chip.

Furniture Witch Flying High

If you happened to attend our son's high school graduation party this past weekend and found his mother choked with emotion, please understand my pain.

We have a new couch, and I was fearful of a spill.

Of course I care about our boy, but I have had 18 years to prepare for the sight of him wearing a mortarboard in public. On the other hand, our new blue couch from Al's has only been in the family for the past two months.

The irony of the situation is, I got the couch because we were having the party. It is part of the longstanding tradition of opening one's home to one's friends, then going to great pains to hide the truth about how one really lives.

"Oh, those windows? They always sparkle and shine! Yes, we varnish and stain every year, just to keep things fresh. What's that? Our teenagers' bedrooms? Uh, sorry. We seem to have lost the keys."

The truth behind our tawdry existence came to light several months ago, as I was cleaning our couch of many colors. Purchased years ago as a pre-owned, it boasted a pattern so unique it defied polite description. Little did we know we were secretly harboring a celebrity.

It turned out our couch had an identical twin, and it was featured in an Ugly Couch Contest on the Regis and Kelly show. The twin lost the contest because even daytime TV has standards, but I didn't allow that to diminish our own couch's claim to fame.

We didn't want it to go to its head cushions, either, so we continued to treat the couch like a regular piece of furniture. We kicked our feet up on it, shooed the dog off it if she was wet, and covered it with a tarp when we had company.

I vacuumed it every once in a while to bring out the natural luster of its fraying fabric. Then, during a recent and tragic grooming session, I looked a little closer and detected a crater in one of its seat cushions.

The exposed foam was a major improvement over the upholstery, but you can't have guests sitting on foam blocks in your living room. They're liable to hold a soup and sandwich benefit. So I turned the cushion over, and discovered an even bigger hole on the other side.

My husband and I would ordinarily react by doing absolutely nothing until we'd been violated by a couch spring. But the graduation party loomed, and the planets must have been lined up just right, because Al's Furniture in Iron River was going out of business.

We beat a path to Al's door, and after careful scrutiny of his rock-bottom deals, picked the price tag we liked best. It was delivered to our home a few days later, attached to a big blue people-eater of a brand new couch.

The couch appears to be of the "puffalump" strain, with plump cushions, a fluffy back and headrest, and arms that could seriously use a workout video. When you sit down, it kind of envelops you, so that only your feet and nose are left showing. Our new couch just loves company.

And I love our new couch, too, so much that hardly anyone is allowed to occupy it. Yes, the Furniture Witch has been flying high since the delivery truck came to our door, to the point where even her cats are afraid to pad across its cushions.

"Did you change your pants before you sat there?" she growls to her husband.

"We eat popcorn in the kitchen now!" she cackles to her children.

"There are shelters in both Houghton and Marquette, you know!" she shrieks as she chases the family pets from the living room.

I knew it had to end the day I found my husband reading his newspaper on the floor in front of the couch. I flicked away a tear (away from the couch, to avoid a spot), put my broom back in the closet and finally mailed out the graduation party invitations.

Three days after the fete, I am happy to report nary a drop nor crumb was spilled on our new blue couch from Al's. That is because nary a guest sat on it. I even guided a few over to it: good, upstanding folk with steady hands and small portions, and they still opted for the folding chairs.

Maybe they just didn't feel comfortable eating on something that threatened to eat them first. Or maybe it was my eye that was twitching as I stood sentry. In any case, I promise to do better when our daughter graduates two years from now.

Though our rust-colored rocker is looking a bit worn...

Secondhand Store Rejection

I knew it was coming, but that didn't ease the blow. I've gotten my first rejection from the secondhand shop.

"Can you still write on that?" the cheerful volunteer asked as I came thumping into the shop, balancing two bulging grocery sacks on a children's blackboard that had gone gray.

"Well, no," I said, easing my bag of socks without partners onto the floor, followed by the Rock-em Sock-em Robots who had learned to get along. "But slap on a little flat black paint, and--"

"Sorry," she said, rather unconvincingly I thought, suspiciously eyeing an argyle paired with a wool hunting sock. "We'd just have to have it hauled away."

Hauled away?! My babies learned to scribble their ABCs on that board, then wipe them off with my good dishtowels. Works of childhood art had once graced its now slippery surface, along with games of tic-tac-toe and house rules that were "accidentally" erased.

In more recent years, it was used to record phone messages, important dates, and wish lists for the designated grocery shopper: first pop and candy, and later, shampoo and razor blades. Then one sad day, the blackboard finally quit taking notes altogether.

What was I thinking? Snatching up the board again and mumbling something about leftover black paint in our garage, I darted out of the shop before the robots and socks had a chance to hitch a ride back with me.

It is hard to accept the fact that your treasures are another person's junk. It's even harder to accept that your junk is not another person's treasures.

The theory is put to the test each spring, when the promise of warm weather sends a strong hint that it is time to take down the Christmas decorations. The tree sheds its last two needles on the way out the door. Without thinking, I stoop to pick them up.

Spring cleaning has officially begun.

Before they can say, "Mom has a problem with Endust," the kids are coming home to gutted bedrooms and neatly arranged closets. Curtains are down, walls are washed, and posters of ill-behaved rock stars have disappeared. Unfortunately, I still hear from them.

Nothing escapes the scrutiny of Mom in spring cleaning mode, who looks a little like the Grim Reaper but bears a mop instead of a scythe. Every drawer is emptied, every note is read, and almost every wad of gum is found in my relentless pursuit of good, clean living.

In the kitchen, cereal boxes are arranged according to height and cans are neatly stacked. Cabinet fronts are scraped free of grime and polished. All the dusty little bottles in the spice rack are still dusty, but their labels now neatly face the front.

The same goes for the medicine cabinet, where old prescriptions are tossed out and old perfume is liberally sampled until I drive myself right out of the bathroom. Then it's on to the mud room, the only room in the house that comes by its name honestly, until it's clean as a foyer.

Pets are chased outside. Kids refuse to come in. Storm chasers circle the block, angling for the perfect shot of the black funnel cloud mysteriously hovering over our son's bedroom. When the dust tornado and scent of Evening in Paris finally settle down, the biggest challenge of all awaits: what to do with all the stuff that didn't make this year's cut?

There's a waffle iron that's guaranteed to stick, heart-shaped frames that look like kidneys and enough bud vases to float the Rose Bowl. Also, clothes the children have grown out of and clothes I'm never going to shrink back into.

By the time the job is done, I have almost a dozen grocery sacks of collectibles just waiting to be redistributed. With a little convincing, all are taken in at the secondhand shop, with the exception of one exceptional blackboard just waiting on some paint.

15. MOM RULES

Scaling Mt. Coffee Grounds

Admitting you have a problem is the first step toward fixing it. When a friend told me last fall that she recycles coffee grounds by tossing them out on her lawn, I followed suit, pitching mine out our kitchen door all winter.

So, what's my problem? Taking bum advice from friends!

By December, the sun wasn't cresting Mt. Coffee Grounds until midday. In January, kids started showing up with their sleds. February brought ski jumpers, and in March we receive a warning from the FAA, something about interfering with flight patterns.

People who spot Mt. Coffee Grounds from land or sky might think I have a problem with coffee. As they say in French Roast, au contraire! I get along great with coffee! It wakes me up! It puts me down! It makes me highly exclamatory because my blood type is C for caffeine!

It all started one day when I was 12 years old and bored. I asked my parents if I could get a puppy? No. Walk to the mall with my friend Cheri? No. Order a unicycle from the Sears catalog? No. Drink coffee? Yeah, why not.

You don't get lucky very often when you're 12, so before my parents could take it back, I poured myself a cup of equal parts cream, sugar, and coffee. I've been a big fan of the brew ever since, minus most of the cream and all of the sugar, or I'd now be as big as Baltimore.

We had one of the first automatic coffee makers at home, a unit that took up a lot more space than a puppy would have but at least you could control the drips. The best part of my new drinking habit was that now my folks had two coffee makers: Bruin and Nancy.

I'd been drinking on the run for almost 10 years when my brother, Jim, taught me how to drink and drive. Jim enlisted in the Air Force, and left me his not-so-gently used '67 Chrysler Newport. Like a horse pulling a milk wagon, it was trained to stop at every coffee counter in town.

It stopped at 7-Elevens and White Castles, and that was about it because they didn't have Starbucks on Chicago's South Side back in the 1970s. They didn't have cup holders in cars, either. Instead, we had St. Christopher medals pasted onto our dashboards.

St. Christopher was the patron saint of travelers, and had a special place in his heart for people who drove with cups of scalding coffee balanced in their laps. He and Jim's car kept me both safe and caffeinated until I left home to get even higher, this time on education.

My drinking habit got worse in college, as drinking habits often do. I drank instant coffee because the Bruin was too big to fit in my dorm room. I sipped Postum with a group of freethinkers. And one especially groggy morning, I accidentally knocked back a cup of decaf with skim milk.

On my car dashboard back at home, St. Christopher shed real tears.

With age comes maturity, and I'm proud to state I have my habit under control. I've even become a bit of a coffee snob. I still drink coffee from gas stations, but only certain gas stations, and then it has to be the highest octane on tap.

When I visit Mom in Wisconsin, I visit Kwik Trip first for a cup of Karuba Dark Roast. Sometimes it takes me a few tries to hit the button, but you can always turn to a decaf drinker for assistance. We coffee drinkers tend to shake, I mean "stick," together.

Between visits to Mom and Kwik Trip, I keep bags of Karuba Dark Roast in the cupboard for times when I need a pick-me-up, a put-me-down, or just another cup of chewy coffee. I don't have a problem. I have a mountain, and a friend that made me create it.

Mom's Commencement Address

Dear graduates,

I am addressing you in print today because quite frankly, no school in its right mind would invite me to take the podium in person. I use bad grammar. I wear my scuffy blue boots for dress. I know 'scuffy" is not a word, yet I typed it anyway.

I have distinguished myself in neither academic nor athletic fields. Twenty-some years ago, I used my B.A. to get to the U.P., and haven't added any initials since. So what, you ask, could I possibly have to say to a highly sophisticated class of graduating high school seniors?

Graduates, I hope you're happy. You are tearing your mothers' hearts right out of their chests!

In the 17, 18-plus years it has taken you to reach this mighty portal, do you have any idea how many tears your mothers have shed watching you grow? "A coupla' cupfuls," you say? "I dunno, maybe a gallon?"

Try a lake!

The doctor cut the cord first, but you have been severing ties ever since. You weaned yourself from your loving mother to a sippy cup, which you used to spill milk all over her house. You dropped her hand to pick up your first tee-ball bat. Then you whacked her with it while she was busy trying to balance your ball on the tee.

You marched off to kindergarten without looking back, even though Mom was trying to be brave. You waved at her when you got your kindergarten diploma, flaunting your independence as she tried to focus on your tear-blurred features. Her tears, not yours.

School assemblies, soccer games, skating shows and proms all moved you by inches and leaps from your mother's arms to where you are now seated. Very soon, you will wave a final goodbye that will break her heart to return. It is the one that means you are all grown up.

Now, before you go off and do that, there are just a few more Mom things I would like to impress upon you today. It is the real reason I am addressing you graduates. Moms like to get the last word in, and these are words you need to hear just one more time.

Mind your manners. When your principal hands you your diploma today, say thank you. Later on, when Mom and Dad take you to a nice restaurant to celebrate your grown-uppedness and the waitress puts your plate in front of you, thank her, too. People deserve your respect.

Say you're sorry. Due to the fact you are not God, you will spend a good percentage of every day screwing up royally. Say you're sorry when you do. When you say it, look the person in the eye. You're not excusing yourself. You're asking that person's forgiveness. If you don't mean it, it doesn't count.

Share. Now that you are an adult, Mom isn't going to tell you, "Tommy, give Danny the keys. It's his turn to drive your Chevy Lumina!" You shared a sandbox with Danny. You know how that kid drove. Share your time and skills, freely and generously, as a volunteer. The best paying jobs don't have a thing to do with money.

Don't say "hate." Hatred topples tall buildings and makes people feel bad. You can hate Brussels sprouts, I guess, but you can't let them hear you say it.

Take care of your brother, and now that you are an adult, everyone is your brother. If someone is hurting, speak up or step in. If you can't, then run for someone who can. Mom is not asking you to be a hero. She is expecting you to behave like a human being.

Spread the love. If you can't, then run for someone who can. Mom joke! Seriously now, today you will get the stuffing hugged out of you. You will also get lots of graduation envelopes to open and shake upside down. Money will buy many college textbooks, but the best gift you'll receive is the love. Give a little of it back to the world each day.

Don't slam doors. Mom got you this far with all 10 fingers intact. From now on, avoiding boo-boos is up to you. A whole lifetime of new jobs and relationships lies ahead. When they end, close the doors gently. If you are very lucky, someday you may be welcomed back in.

Do your homework. If you think you are done with homework just because you are a high school graduate, then Mom is not the only one who suffered a head injury in tee-ball. Homework is college chemistry. It's also balancing the checkbook and painting the eaves. Work first, then play.

Well, I had better get back to my homework now, too. It includes dusting off this podium for someone who listened better than I did in algebra. But before I do that, I have just one more Mom thing to say.

Don't miss the bus.

You've been getting ready for it for over 12 years now, and the future just turned down your road. It's filled with people you never dreamed of meeting, and opportunities that won't wait long for you to hop on board. It brings joys beyond belief, and sometimes, more pain than you thought you could ever endure.

But you can, because you are your mother's child.

Flying Wallendas Grounded

I am not one to throw caution to the wind. I prefer direct delivery. "Be careful on those monkey bars."

"Be careful not to spill your juice."

"Be careful you don't kick Grandma when she's pushing you on the swi-OOF!"

I was fine, just a little muddy, but I cannot overemphasize the importance of always being careful. There are people in the world who don't know the meaning of fear. Most of them are safely buried.

The rest live to give me even more gray hairs, or, in the case of the Flying Wallendas, lively entertainment. That's because the Flying Wallendas are not my grandchildren. If they were, they'd all be grounded.

Allow me to explain. One of my favorite childhood books was about saints. It was a gift to my older brother from his godfather, who was a priest, and was probably meant to inspire little Bobby to stop whaling on little Nancy.

It didn't take. Instead, Nancy read Bobby's saint book while hiding from him, usually under the dining room table. It became my very favorite book, and it was there that I learned saints lived good and pure lives and were usually martyred.

The Flying Wallendas have nothing over the Swinging Grandson, except for glittery costumes and some major altitude. If I had been their grandmother, I'd have grounded them.

Then I looked up "martyred," and found a new favorite book.

It was the story of the Flying Wallendas, a family of circus performers. Their troupe traveled all over Europe performing as acrobats. And they usually ended up a lot better than those saints did, unless they happened to slip.

That's how they earned their name, from a mishap that once sent four Wallendas flying. They landed relatively unscathed, but many since have been injured and some even killed because of what the Flying Wallendas won't do: use safety nets.

It is a family tradition, like making hay except nobody would pay to see that. Wallendas start out small, even younger than the grandchild who leaves footprints on my chest, typically taking to the heights before kindergarten.

I wouldn't read a book without the protection of the dining room table, and little Wallendas were flying through the air without so much as a mattress to land on! It boggled my mind. Or maybe I'd just bumped my head too hard under the table.

Fast forward about 50 years, to a sunny afternoon with my husband at the U.P. State Fair. The livestock had been duly admired, hogs in particular because they have personality plus. Displays of crafts and produce evoked their usual notes of envy, and nearby, deep fried elephant ears caught my eye.

But "Circus Incredible" was about to begin, one of several free shows offered on the midway, so we headed for the bleachers. A man and two women in glittery leotards took their bows, then proceeded to break every safety rule I've ever preached.

All around us, people who weren't raised better egged them on. The man balanced on a tall tower. Then he added more height. Next he added a wobbly cylinder, and more objects, each time asking the audience's opinion of his going even higher.

I gave him mine, loud and clear, but was drowned out by a sea of approval. He finally dismounted, bowed again, then introduced the mother/daughter team that would take utter carelessness to whole new heights.

First Mom did some very irresponsible acrobatics high on a rope. Then her daughter, suspended by her ankles, spun her mom in fast, tight circles on a strap around both of their necks. Many feet below, there was no safety net to catch either one if they fell.

The biggest thrill, though, was yet to come. At the end of the show, the man casually introduced his two partners as sixth and seventh generation Flying Wallendas. I had seen my childhood heroes perform live, right in the U.P.! And I lived to write about it!

I may have even clapped a little. Saints preserve us.

Judge Nancy's Got No Appeal

The government wants us to interpret the Bible literally!

Not all of it. Nobody's going to believe Noah actually invited two mosquitoes onto the ark to insure the propagation of those little blood-sucking devils. No, I am talking about just one passage, and it's "Spare the rod and spoil the child."

That's right. Some legislator wants to pass a law that makes it illegal to spank children ages four and under in California. When they reach the legal age of five, you can apparently dust them off to your heart's delight.

The politician's reason for taking this stand was that it would buy her lots of morning news airtime. Also, she thinks spanking (the "s" word) is very bad. Reportedly, it is a belief she shares with Dr. Phil, Super Nanny, and Sweden.

I am not about to type the words "spanking is good" because that would set me up for a lot of nasty letters. Nasty letters are bad. Instead, I will explore reasons why good parents spank bad children.

Personally speaking, HA! Nice try! I am not about to lose custody of my beloved children by admitting I broke a future law in California. Instead I will type about fictitious friends who spanked our, I mean "their" children so they wouldn't spoil. They spanked their children when they ignored the rules, endangering themselves or others. They spanked when their children assumed too much authority for their tender ages, then wielded it badly. They spanked their children so they'd grow up straight.

Pain was never the objective. For a child, it was an insult to have your size 4T overalls dusted in front of your buddies in the sandbox. Especially by a woman old enough to be your mother. Because she was your mother.

Spanking worked. Sand quit flying in peoples' faces, and dump trucks got back on the job making roads instead of going airborne. As a result, especially if the dump truck was made of metal, nobody needed stitches. Or therapy either, for that matter.

Of course, by the time little ones reached the age of reason, spanking was no longer an effective disciplinary tool. When our own children came of age, we guided them with common sense, sometimes delivered in a voice that could shatter glass.

Oh, the fun we had raising our children right! If they ran in the store, they had to sit in the cart. If they didn't stay by Mom on a hike in the woods, they had to walk behind her. The view alone was punishment enough.

If they hurt someone, they had to stand beside the patient while Mom cleaned the wound and mopped up tears, often both the victim's and the perpetrator's. Then they had to apologize to the victim, and administer a hug.

If they broke someone's toy, they had to replace it. If they said something bad about someone, they had to say three good things about him or her. The compliments alone made the sentence worthwhile.

"I like her hair. It's kind of stringy."

"This meatloaf is better than your Spanish rice.

"He knows more swears than anyone else on the playground!"

The crowning glory of our days of disciplining children was my short but memorable stint as the Honorable Judge Mom. I took my oath of duty at the end of a long day of domestic squabbles. My term on the bench lasted less than an hour.

The children had been pestering me all day long to settle arguments over toys, TV shows, personal boundaries, etc. I finally got fed up with it, and announced if I had to serve as judge, I would henceforth and therefore be charging 25 cents per judgment.

I would serve as both judge and jury, and decisions could not be appealed. Neither could the cost, no matter which way my judgment went.

I had already cleared 50 cents when a plaintiff approached with a quarter in her little mitt and a complaint against her brother. I graciously accepted my pay, heard her case, then passed judgment in favor of the defendant.

"But I paid you!" she squealed.

"But he's right," I said. "Judgment stands!"

I hung up my robe and have been slaving as a mother and journalist ever since. But for what it's worth, exactly two bits, I'd still rule in favor of the "s" word.

Our Grandchild, the Weimaraner

Nature can play such cruel tricks. Like our first grandchild, Zoey.

Zoey has a big nose and a tendency to drool. She has gangly legs and short, silvery hair. Her mother is hesitant to cut baby's toenails, so they click on the linoleum whenever Zoey runs around the house.

Did I mention Zoey is a Weimaraner? That's right, our first grandchild is a German. And a real hound dog, too.

Since time immemorial, it has been the practice of young people to hone their nurturing skills first on pets, then on real live human grandbabies. About the time their parents start cooing and fussing over babies in restaurants and sighing at newborn clothing displays, their kids drop the bomb:

"We're getting a dog!"

A dog is a fine start to a family. It guards the house and warms the hearth. It chases the squirrels and the mailman. It teaches responsibility to our children, and offers hope for an even greater good in the future. Like real live human grandbabies.

To their credit, our daughter Katy and her boyfriend Matt scanned area shelters in their search for the perfect fit. They wanted a bigger dog with shorter hair that didn't shed much, and looked high and low for just the right pet. What they got was Zoey.

According to literature I tracked down after the blessed arrival, the Weimaraner is a sporting dog "originally bred and disciplined by the autocrats of the Weimar province of Germany some hundred years ago."

But wait—it gets even better!

"The Weimaraner is a superb example of a breed in which only the best was considered good enough. At one time it was hard to get because enthusiasts guarded their breed's reputation zealously, but is now plentiful."

I may be just a mutt—Irish, English, Scotch, Bohemian, Danish, and German at last count—but if our little Zoey is a superb example of only the best, some German autocrat from Weimar has a lot of explaining to do.

Like why does Zoey, who weighs about 60 pounds and can rest her chin on Grandma's kitchen table while dolefully eyeing the cookie plate, have to sleep with her head covered?

Ever since her first night at her new home, Zoey has consistently left the comfort of her dog bed to sneak under the people bedcovers.

One night she got stuck at the foot of the bed where she whined miserably until re-directed toward the light.

We have never allowed pets on our furniture, unless those pets are cats that begrudgingly allow us on their furniture. Zoey is not only welcome on the kids' couches, but you have to hold her blanket up so she can crawl under it, too, with only her tail sticking out. Unless it's too cold for tail exposure.

Did I mention our Zoey is wonderful with children? When Matt's niece, a delightful toddler named Rylee, climbs onto the couch atop Zoey, the big silver hound responds with both dignity and grace: a deep sigh issues from under the toddler on the blanket on the dog on the couch.

Grandma was absent for the big event, but I guess Zoey was not too enthralled with her first snowfall. She galloped twice around the backyard, ears and droopy chops flapping in the wind, then skidded to a stop on the porch and looked balefully to my daughter to let her back in and under her blanket.

Zoey loves to go for car rides, curled up in the backseat, preferably under her blanket. When she visits Grandma and Grandpa in the country, she tears through the house straight to the middle bedroom to watch her favorite TV show, starring Molly the guinea pig.

We inherited Molly from our daughter Gwen because the Air Force does not issue uniforms to guinea pigs. That's Gwen's story and she's sticking to it. I might be a grandmother to a Weimaraner, but I refuse to claim blood ties to a rodent. Molly is a distant relative, several times removed.

Zoey will spend a whole afternoon staring into Molly's cage. Molly, who is usually quite timid, will climb up on her feeding shelf to allow an even closer look. Sometimes it's just too much for Zoey, who will thump Molly's cage with her oversize nose in the interest, I think, of eating the star of the show.

Well, I am not the kind of grandma who is going to let my little Weimaraner vegetate in front of a TV. I shut the dog out of the room, disappointing both animals until I fold like yesterday's wash and let the big galoot back in. It is a grandma's due. You spoil 'em, then send 'em back home again.

My husband, who would like our grandchild better if she was a bird dog but loves Zoey anyway, cannot even pronounce the word

"Weimaraner," proof positive I didn't marry an autocrat. He calls her a "Weimaraneraneraner," kind of like a German police siren.

With the holiday season fast approaching, Katy is threatening yet another shock to Grandma's delicate system. She and Matt want me to take a photo of them with Zoey in ugly Christmas sweaters for a family Christmas card.

Uncle Sam has a hand in it too, after purchasing three hideous sweaters, His & Hers & Dog's, from Goodwill last week. I can't complain too loudly, because I've already got dibs on Katy's sweater after the photo shoot. Wearing ugly Christmas sweaters is another of Grandma's dues.

I don't fully approve—I fear a snag in my future sweater if the flash spooks Zoey—but at least I'll finally have a photo to share when my peers whip out the latest shots of their grandchildren.

"This is our little Zoey!" I'll proudly proclaim, displaying a shot of the lovable hound dog sporting her ugly knit vest with the reindeer motif. "She's a German!"

16. GENDER SPECIFICS

We're Pols Apart

"It smelled so bad, Dr. Pol had to share."

The preceding sentence says a lot. It says I watch *The Incredible Dr. Pol,* a TV show about a gruff but lovable old-school country veterinarian. It says men will be boys. And most important, (see quotation marks), it says I didn't say it first.

Dr. Jan Pol is a Dutch-American veterinarian in his mid-70s with a practice based in Weidman, MI. He has an accent thick as spring mud, and originated the popular practice of cow tipping.

Actually, he flips 'em out in the barnyard, then sews one of their stomachs back into place, right through their thick hides after untwisting their guts. It's not exactly poetry in motion, but it's great entertainment.

Unless you happen to be the cow.

We like Pol because he is just like our former country vet, Dr. Talsma, except for the accent. Years ago, when we brought in a stray cat that had lost its argument with a farm dog, Talsma scrutinized its multiple piercings and administered a big shot of antibiotic.

"If it works, he'll live," Talsma said. "If it doesn't, he won't."

He lived! And then he strayed a few farms over, where he continued to incur large medical bills for bad choices; but the point is, Dr. Talsma saved the cat at minimal expense and even fewer words. He was also a big hit with our three kids, showing them how to use a cow syringe as a whistle.

Talsma is retired now, and the cow syringe whistle has long since disappeared, but we can still enjoy Pol's antics on Saturday mornings. While improving his patients' conditions, he speaks volumes about the human one.

That big bad smell Pol shared came from a tiny hedgehog. A woman brought the beloved pet in because it was suffering from a bad ear infection. The patient proved so prickly it curled into a ball and wouldn't unwind to be examined.

So Pol put it under, then very nearly joined it.

The smell from its ears just about knocked Pol off his feet. When he recovered, he called in his office staff, all of them women, to take a whiff, resulting in a stampede for the exit followed by thickly accented laughter.

And at the expense of sounding ever so slightly sexist, that is so like a guy!

When it comes to all things down and dirty, guys just love to share. If a guy takes a hit, especially if it lands below the belt, his fellow men/boys will typically hit the dirt alongside him because they are laughing too hard to continue standing upright.

If a woman goes down for any reason whatsoever—softball injury, broke a heel, broke up with her boyfriend—the sisterhood instinctively moves in for a group hug.

If I catch a slimy northern pike while my sister-in-law Joan is rowing, I politely keep it a safe distance from her spotless sneakers, which are usually drawn up onto her boat seat, anyway.

If my ice fishing partner, Barry, hooks a burbot, which is an eel-like species that was a front runner for the lead role in "Alien," he will toss it over my head and out the shanty door, spraying me in a shower of slime along the way.

Because it's so awful, he has to share.

Men Are From Mud

It's spring, when a young man's fancy lightly turns to thoughts of getting stuck in the mud.

That's how the poem would have read if Alfred, Lord Tennyson had been born in the U.P. Instead, he was born in England and wrote "thoughts of love," securing his place in classic English Literature but pretty much spinning his wheels in terms of local lore.

Men are naturally attracted to mud. As small children, they delight in watching mud puddles swallow their boots. Then they holler for Mom to tug them free again, and re-engage before she can even get back to the house.

As adults, men delight in burying their ATVs in mud holes. Then they proudly post a video on the internet, and message their friends to come tug them free again. They post that video, too.

I do not mean any of the above in a derogatory manner. I mean it as a woman who has experienced firsthand the roar of an engine, the spinning of all four tires and the wet slap of airborne mud as her date's vehicle goes down for the count.

Take-backs! I am totally slamming men everywhere, even ones in suits and ties who visit car washes regularly, for their oneness with mudder earth. Quoting yet another writer who's better than me, "God formed man of the dust of the ground" (Genesis 2:7).

And he's been determined to get back to his roots ever since (Nancy 4/20).

Women have a mixed relationship with mud. When we're little, it's good for making mud pies. Then we discover Easy Bake Ovens that crank out pies we can actually eat, and we're pretty much over cooking with mud.

When we're big, mud feels good on our faces at the spa, but only because we don't have to do the spa's laundry. If we did, we'd finish our own facials with a squeegee. We willingly dig in the mud to plant flower bulbs and vegetable starts and retrieve toddlers' boots, but there is one thing women of all ages just cannot abide.

We don't like to get left in the mud.

The story as old as the dust of the ground played out at our own home just a short time ago. Our son, Sam, took his two-year-old niece Natalie for an ATV ride. Upon their return, the previously adoring toddler had daggers in her eyes.

"'Tuck!" she cried, wringing her chubby little fingers together to mimic getting stuck with her uncle on his ATV. "'Tuck!"

"Just like a woman!" he said in disgust. "Get 'em stuck and right away, they start cryin'!" Apparently, she started to howl the minute his wheels started to spin. Adding insult to injury, he bumped her with his butt while getting off the ATV, sending her sprawling. To our delight, she later added the word "butt" to her narrative.

She got a cookie. He caught h---. Too bad there's not a video.

Demand Pink Reform

Women of America, raise a hand.

Now make a fist and bring it down really hard, making sure not to make a mess you'd have to clean up later, because we are fighting mad about Pink Taxes.

If you are not quite sure what you're so mad about, Pink Taxes are the difference in cost between men's and women's products. In some instances, it is estimated as high as 42 percent.

And can you guess who the victims are?

If you answered, "Your readers," you are a real wisenheimer. It's women! Starting at birth when we are color-coded with little pink caps, women are programmed to think pink, and it makes the corporate world see green.

Pink razor blades cost more than blue ones. Women's shampoo costs more than men's. Women's deodorant costs more, too, though in the end we smell like "Secret Ocean Escape" while men get the "Axe."

Please pardon my gender discrimination, but I have paid dearly for it, to the tune of a whopping $1,351 annually if you can believe my laptop. I'd feel better about it if it was pink, but I couldn't swing the price difference.

The evidence is beyond dispute. Little girls' bicycle helmets designed to look like a shark cost $27.99. Boys' shark helmets cost just $14.99. Women's bladder pads ring up the same as men's, but we get a dozen less pads for the price.

Again, I should not be so bold in print, especially on the subject of bladder pads, but women clearly need to stand together against the injustice of Pink Taxes. And nobody wants to stand beside someone who got shortchanged on her bladder pads.

There are several theories why women pay more than men for similar products. One is that we enjoy shopping, two is that we shop more, and three, we are willing.

I am thinking the list was compiled by someone who gets his toiletries on the cheap.

I cannot explain the anomaly of overpriced bicycle helmets and bladder pads, except to say they get us coming and going, but I can tell you here and now why women tend to pay more for personal care products: we have our own aisles, and we need to hit them fast.

When women are young, our carts contain small children who would prefer to free range. We can contain them for only so long before they dissolve into puddles of tears, ruining all the Pink Taxed items for which we are paying so dearly.

When women are older, our cars contain bored husbands waiting outside the store who would prefer to drive home and watch TV.

And they would do it, too, except eventually they'd dearly miss all the stuff we're busy buying them for 42 percent less.

Knowledge is power, and if you can believe my non-pink laptop, we need to wield it wisely by making more manly choices (blue razors, boy sharks) (but never, ever Axe) and calling our congressmen to demand Pink Tax reform.

They'll appreciate the company while they're waiting out in their cars.

Don't Touch His Tees

The secret to a long and happy marriage is not love.

It is not communication.

It is not sex.

It is respecting your husband's right to wear t-shirts with just enough fabric left to hold them together, then scowling fiercely at people on the street who keep trying to tuck spare change into his travel mug.

If you think I am being cruel and heartless, you are a husband. If you have ever had to attach one end of a winch to the windowsill and the other to the handle of an overstuffed rotten t-shirt drawer, just so you can stuff another rotten t-shirt in it, you are a wife.

It is purely conjecture, but I am fairly sure these roles were set in stone shortly after Eve bit the apple. Gathering several shrubs in complementing shades of green around her newly naked form and accessorizing with a nice ivy cap, Eve cast a long look at Adam and said, "You're not wearing *that* tired old fig leaf, are you?"

From that time on, women have been fighting an uphill battle to get their husbands to discard clothing that has seen better decades. The problem is that men are comfortable in their skin. And they are not afraid to reveal a few yards of it through the remains of their old high school football jerseys.

Women also cling to favorite items of clothing, but we wouldn't dream of wearing them in public. In the U.P., it is the real reason we settle in underpopulated areas and plant our gardens a safe distance from the road and occasional traffic. We have our dignity.

And I have my Morris the Cat t-shirt.

Morris was a promotional item Dad brought home from work shortly after Eve redressed Adam. The real Morris died years ago, but his washed-out, ripped-up mug still sneers up at me from a corner of my t-shirt drawer. Morris has a reason for being. He reminds me of my dad.

I also have the same jogging pants that saw me through the first half, first quarter, and first two weeks of three pregnancies. I'd wear them to weed the garden, but our meter man would start estimating our bill and UPS would leave our packages with the neighbors.

Except for the truly special clothing items, like dead cat tees and rotten joggers, women are usually all too ready to part with old clothes so we can go shopping for new ones. Conversely, men believe all items of clothing appreciate with wear, and that less really is more.

The proof is in the racks of men's t-shirts at our local thrift store. Most of the tees are in mint condition, with nary a hole nor grease spot on them. That is why they are not being bought by men.

If the store emptied its racks on Main Street one morning and allowed traffic to walk, roll, and grind across the tees until closing time, then gathered them up and re-hung them, L'Anse could boast its first designer men's clothing shop.

The problem is, men still wouldn't shop there because they already have a drawer full of rotten t-shirts at home.

While men may appear casual about burying their treasures in overstuffed drawers, they never lose their preternatural connection to their most user-friendly tees. It is almost like a mother and child relationship, but not really.

I could fuel a campfire with my husband's good suit, his dress shirt and slacks, and he'd unwittingly roast a marshmallow over the flames and inquire about my day. If I use one of his t-shirt remnants as a dust rag, he's on the phone to Judge Judy.

Just a few short weeks ago, I was sorting through my husband's dresser drawers, plucking out winter wear for summer storage. When I got to his shirt drawer, I grabbed up some flannels, then found a ragged t-shirt collar that still had one sleeve attached.

I lovingly folded it and carefully put it back in his drawer. This October, not necessarily in style, we will celebrate our 20th wedding anniversary.

17. COOK'S CHOICE

Fame Finds Me

I am hoping fame will not change me but it already has because I feel compelled to thank all the little people who helped me make it big in "Yooper Bars."

No, I am not talking about the U.P.-imprinted candy bars made by Sayklly's. I wish it was the candy. I am talking about a book about actual bars in the U.P. My mug is pictured inside, grinning out for all the world and my grandchildren to someday see.

And on Sept. 6, 2015, the book was featured in *The New York Times*.

I got the scoop from my friend and partner in crime, Deb Nelson. She's pictured, too, and wrote me just last week to say we'd finally made the bigs in a little old bar in Copper Harbor.

Nance—in the 9/6/15 Sunday New York Times *travel section there's a full-page article titled, "One Father, One Son and 109 Bars" about the self-published book, "Yooper Bars." We have made the big time!!! I was trying to impress my co-workers with this. I mean, it's* THE NEW YORK TIMES *with the difficult crossword puzzles, but no one has yet asked for an autographed copy...*

Sorry, no autographs today. I'm much too busy trying to formulate future alibis for when the grandkids ask about my past. But just between you and me, once upon a time my husband Don and I and our friends, Mark and Deb Nelson, were approached for a photo in Zik's Bar by someone claiming to write a book.

Of course we smiled for his camera! We like books!

And we like Zik's, an establishment that endeared itself to us years ago by sponsoring an Air Guitar Contest. My husband and I witnessed it on our annual fall color tour, which can happen any time of year because Zik's is a very colorful establishment, but that time it was actually fall.

The bar was filled to its dusty rafters with rollicking patrons and make-believe musicians, and the competition was fierce. One lady even had a back-up band of an air drum, an air bass player, and someone who was probably just trying to find the bathroom.

Another contestant laid on his back on the pool table, twitching and kicking his feet in the air while he strummed at his belly button. He might have needed the bathroom too, or maybe medical attention, but we all clapped politely when he was done and then the pool players got back to their game.

Zik's was the hottest ticket in Copper Harbor that night, and nobody was actually playing music. Sammy, the guy who owned the bike shop across the street, took home the imaginary trophy. Then they cranked up the juke box again and it was business as usual.

And my husband and I kept going back for more, exactly one night of every year. Then we introduced Mark and Deb to Zik's charms, the same night authors Randy and Kevin Kluck were cruising the establishment for an article in their guide to U.P. bars.

We were playing a spirited game of pool because we are incapable of playing a skilled one. The girls were winning because Deb, who is an accountant, has been fixing the girls' scores since our children were little. Our families would play rousing games of kickball, dads & boys vs. moms & girls, and girls always won by five.

A man came up between shots (pool shots, that is) and started chatting about a book. It sounded like a line to me—who writes about Zik's?—but we all smiled for a photo and then returned to our game of beating the men by five. And we never heard another word about it.

Until the following Christmas, when our family was gathered at the home of our daughter, Katy and her husband, Matt, for dinner and a gift exchange. There was a lovely spread, glasses of cheer, a beaming grandchild at my knee, and a little book-shaped package on the table before me.

"Open it, Mom," Katy said with a twinkle in her eye, kind of like Saint Nick minus the Saint. Lo and behold, there gleamed before me "Yooper Bars," a guide to bars in the U.P., with page 187 clearly marked because Mom and Dad and Mark and Deb were pictured right at the top of it.

It seems the book was on sale locally at the CueMaster in Baraga, which is also featured in "Yooper Bars," and the kids' friend, Joe

Linder, spotted us inside. The photo is extremely small, not much bigger than a postage stamp, but we were clearly busted.

I tried to tuck the book under my new Christmas dish towels, but I'd been outed. It made the rounds of the room to much laughter and personal blushing, then was relegated to a dark bookshelf in our home until last week when I got the heads-up from Deb.

I dug it out again this past weekend, and discovered the House Drink at Zik's is not my usual, Busch Light. It's Copper Harbor Sunset, a concoction that might make you regret the Copper Harbor sunrise the next day. There's a Best Joke at Zik's, too, but you won't read it here.

The Fact or Fiction section of the article struck a chord when it noted Zik's is the "official meeting place when there's a power outage in Copper Harbor. They may not have a generator, but they do have drinks and companionship."

I finally got the Air Guitar Contest.

Lights Out in Watton

I'm kind of glad I'm going in to work today, because if I were at home, I'd be absolutely powerless.

By "powerless" I don't mean like Superman in the presence of Kryptonite, or Iron Man when his suit is out for dry cleaning. No, this is much more serious. I'd be without electricity.

The terrifying news arrived just a few weeks ago in the form of an innocent looking letter from WE Energies. On Tuesday, Nov. 13, our power would be shut off from 9 a.m. to 2 p.m. for maintenance. Sorry for any inconvenience. Have a nice day.

I felt a tightening in my chest, possibly linked to that burrito from Taco Bell last night with two packets of Diablo sauce. But a coronary could not be entirely ruled out because our power company was going to pull the plug on us, and for five long hours, life as we know it would hang in the balance.

Here's how I know it: I get up at roughly any hour of the morning because sometime between 0-60, I apparently forgot how to sleep. I look at the clock to see what time today is starting. The glowing, oversize digital numbers inform me it's still bedtime, you idiot. Go back to sleep.

My clock is not the boss of me. My bladder is the boss of me. So I head for the powder room and switch on the light so I can powder my nose. Then I head into the kitchen and switch on the light so I can locate my coffee pot.

I pour a shot of yesterday's brew and reheat it in the microwave. I open the refrigerator and add a splash of cream to neutralize the high octane. Then I head for the living room and my favorite corner of the couch, switch on the lamp, and plug in my laptop so I can do some writing.

I also plug in my craft store Christmas tree, crafted to resemble a toilet brush, so I can bask in the glow of whatever lights are still working. In my defense, I know Christmas is still over a month away, but the season of lights has been cut by five long hours.

WE Energies said so.

Modern man and woman were not made to stumble in the darkness with a cup of cold coffee in hand. We have come too far to go back to those days of yore when you had to wind yore clock by hand, then light a candle to find out it was just 2:38 a.m.

The candle would light your way to the outhouse, because you couldn't charge the battery on your reciprocating saw to cut a hole in your floor for a toilet. Back inside, you'd have to add wood to the stove to reheat your coffee, then go outside again to politely ask the cow to add some cream.

The candle would light your way back to the house again and to the couch, where you would take a knife-sharpened pencil in hand and get some writing done. But first, you'd have to light the candles on the toilet brush tree, which would consequently burn the house down with you in it.

By "you" I of course mean "me," and I am thanking my lucky un-singed britches at this time, which is now 3:42 a.m., that by 9 a.m. I will be seated in a cozy office, a cup of hot coffee in hand, trying to make sense of all this in the light of day while Watton lies in darkness.

Unless the office got a letter from WE Energies, too.

Convoyyyyyy

We've got a mighty convoy, rockin' through the night
Yeah we've got a mighty convoy, ain't we a beautiful sight?

Funny, the things that go through your mind when you're rocketing down the Iowa Interstate in a thick fog at 4:30 a.m. Like, "Was that song really a hit when I was young?" and "If I lose my daughter's taillights, will I ever see home again?"

Yes and yes, though it was a close call after my back-up GPS took a nosedive off the dashboard and went blank just out of town. That's when I knew that if I couldn't follow the light, I'd be banished to the darkness: it would be dark, and I'd be lost in Iowa.

Everyone is born with an inner compass. That doesn't mean they all work. The daughter I was following can wander our woods and find her way home again. I can, too, but only because my husband left some wire on the fence line and it tends to snag my jacket as I barrel by, hopelessly lost.

I suspect that when settlers once wandered the earth, the great prairie was fairly littered with the bones of my ancestors who also lacked direction. It wasn't their fault that the wagons in front of them didn't come with taillights.

Somehow, enough of us survived to hand down the bad gene. Most settled in the city where their commuter trains were firmly affixed to tracks. Those who couldn't commute by train wisely bought bus passes.

Then one day, a brave new journalist from Chicago, IL bid her parents "Yee ha!" and headed south to the U.P. She corrected herself at the end of the alley, headed north, and didn't stop until her front wheels nudged the shore of Lake Superior.

I haven't strayed far from well-beaten paths since, except for last Christmas when our daughter, son-in-law, and grandbaby needed two drivers to help them move up north from Iowa. I bravely volunteered my husband and our son. Then our son found out he had to work.

Was there still enough time to string wire from Iowa to Michigan?

That's just foolishness. Modern man doesn't need wire to keep his wife from free ranging. All he needs is a mighty convoy of a U-Haul truck and three cars with Ma tucked safely in the middle and their daughter riding herd on her from the front.

The trouble started as soon as I got behind the wheel. I plugged in my carefully programmed GPS, placed it on the dashboard, and my car started beeping at me. I finally figured out it was reading the heavy suitcase beside me as a passenger, and wanted it safely secured.

I belted the suitcase in nice and snug, positioned my hands at 10 and 2 on the wheel and waited for my daughter's car ahead of me to pull out. After a couple minutes, my husband got out of the car ahead of me and angrily informed me she'd already left.

I peeled out around his car, disconnecting and dumping the GPS onto the floor in the process, and caught up a block later. We sedately threaded our way through town to the interstate. Then my daughter switched gears to "blastoff," and I was suddenly rocketing along at 70 mph with a broken inner compass and a blank GPS.

Convoyyy... Convoyy...

She tried to call me on my TracFone, but I was so rattled I didn't know which way was up. I literally held the phone upside down and bellowed, "HELLO? HELLO?" Then I spun it around and tried again, only to hear a soft sigh followed by a dial tone.

So I threw my upside down phone on the floor beside my useless GPS.

Considering the time of year, December, we were actually blessed with just light rain and fog, but I wasn't counting my blessings that morning. I was counting my pulse beating through the vein bulging on my forehead, because I felt like the tail of a comet.

I white-gripped my steering wheel and leaned forward to see better. When I foolishly took my eyes off the road (blinked), the taillights would gain a little ground and grow dimmer, causing me to surge ahead at a comfortable speed. FOR AN ASTRONAUT!

Pardon my outburst. I'm still re-adjusting to gravity. Dawn came slowly, probably because we were rocketing away from the sun, but by 8 a.m. we had partial light. I finally made contact with the car's backrest. I even turned on the radio. I was that brave.

The rest of the trip was pretty mundane. We stopped in Madison, WI, to let the baby toddle around and socialize, and again in Eagle River, WI, for a burger before the home stretch. Twelve hours after departure, we dropped the kids off in Negaunee, MI then continued on home.

My daughter was even braver than me, keeping a toddler buckled and sane on a 12-hour drive with a dog and a cat on board and a lunatic alternately lagging and surging behind her. She's a USAF veteran who's been to Iraq and back, but she truly earned her wings the day she guided Mom home from Iowa.

Now, if I could only find my way home from our woods.

Fit in at FinnFest

The excitement has been building since St. Urho said, "Did you see that bug jump?" and now FinnFest is finally upon us. As the U.P. fills to overflowing with people who say "Paiva Paiva" right to your face ("hello" in Finn—who knew?), the rest of us are left with the daunting task of trying to fit in.

I have been a fugitive from ethnicity since birth. I grew up in a Lithuanian neighborhood on Chicago's South Side, where many of the residents were first-generation Americans. In a kingdom of Apanaviciuses, Janusaitises and Butkeviciuses, I was a lowly Irish/English/Danish mix named Emerson.

The children I grew up with were mostly blue-eyed blondes, and their Lithuanian language was quite guttural, at least when it was directed toward me. In 21 years I learned little of the vocabulary, but I knew when some kid hollered, "Kapusta galva!" I'd just been called a cabbage head. Again.

And so my move to the U.P., where many of the children are blue-eyed blondes and the Finnish language is quite guttural, was not so big a stretch as one might think. In the years since, I have learned a thing or two about Finnish culture that might prove helpful to other mutts like me this weekend.

First, Finnish genes are dominant. If you fall in love with and marry a Finn this festive weekend, odds are your kids will be welcomed with open arms when you return to your Lithuanian neighborhood for a visit. You, on the other hand, will still be a kapusta galva.

If you're not familiar with the Finnish language, well, don't expect me to teach it to you, you Paiva Paiva. It has taken years of careful observation and unfailing attention to detail for me to string together a simple sentence like: "Piika, go sauna! We're going Houghton soon!"

(Translation: "Little girl, take a bath! We're going Houghton soon!").

If form matters more than content, and you don't care what you're saying in Finn as long as it sounds good, then here's another helpful hint: the accent is always on the first syllable, as in SIsu, SAUna, BARaga, and SO forth.

I have met Finns who can speak the language so lightly and delicately, you'd swear they were speaking Finn in French. I personally prefer to play it safe, and always bring my sledge along when I know some Finn is expected of me. Why just hit a syllable when you can hammer it home?

You'll want to hang onto your r's for awhile, too, at least long enough to scare cats away, and don't forget to pronounce every letter you encounter. There are some quiet Finns, but none of them exist in the Finnish alphabet.

If you have crossed several continents on foot to attend FinnFest, battling disease, pestilence, and a stubborn summer cold, you may humbly admit, "I came a-ways." Understatement is the very foundation of the Finnish culture, and I've got the story to prove it.

One day, after my Finnish husband and I had already split a forest full of wood, I ventured to inquire, "How many more chunks?" He replied, "A couple." Since that fateful day, I've known a couple days is three weeks, a couple inches is almost two feet, and the legal drinking age is a couple years.

It is an endearing trait, and probably the real reason so many Finns are festing in the U.P. this weekend. Generations ago, Finnish settlers slogged through deep snow in April to get to the co-op, and after purchasing a postcard with "Greetings from the U.P.!" on it, penned this simple message home:

"A few bugs last summer. Winter hangs on a bit. Got a couple inches of snow today."

Have fun at FinnFest!

Yooperman Saves Our Day

Every time a new superhero arrives on the big screen, I cannot help but think I should have gotten butter on my popcorn. Also, that the U.P. could really use a superhero.

The last time the U.P. had a superhero to look up to, it was Paul Bunyan, and I'm pretty sure he hailed from Minnesota. Paul cut quite a swath through the mighty Northwoods with his super size ax and his faithful sidekick, Babe the Blue Ox.

He also stomped all over Minnesota and left holes that secured its title as Land of 10,000 Lakes. I know, because we once spent a night by a lake in Minnesota, zipped in a tent with three active children while a cloud of blood-sucking mosquitoes pummeled the walls trying to get in.

As we all know, superheroes are not born at either Portage View in Hancock or Marquette General. They are born out of adversity. Superman lost his planet and fell out of the sky. Iron Man was blown up by his dad's own Stark Industries inventory. Spider Man got bitten by a spider.

There's one in every crowd. And that's why there's new hope for us, thanks to the superhero contrived this very a.m. at Besonen

Industries, with snow pummeling my office window as I dreamed of future family camping trips in arid regions.

His name? Yooperman!

Borrowing heavily from a formula that obviously works, Yooperman is born on a distant planet populated by wildly handsome men. I guess the women are good looking too. Something threatens its destruction, I am thinking Minnesota mosquitoes, so his parents send him off into space.

In serious need of a diaper change (grandmas think about such things), he plummets to earth where he lands on a farmer's rock fence in Michigan's U.P. There he is never seen again, because U.P. rock fences are permanent depositories for scrap metal that might someday come in handy.

That is what you call a "plot twist." Actually, the baby IS found because the price of scrap metal is up! The scrap dealer won't accept babies, so the farmer raises him as his own, teaching him to be a moral and upstanding American even though he will someday wear spandex in public.

Like all superheroes before him, the boy is very strong and can fly. He can top-load the hay wagon without breaking a sweat, hoe the farmer's fields in five minutes flat, and pull his pickup out of a snowbank with one hand, because even Yooperman gets stuck in the U.P.

His nickname? "Scrappy."

The thing about your superheroes is, they need their villains or they just wind up collecting unemployment, and it takes a lot of assistance to feed a blue ox. The villains should also be visually disturbing, like The Joker or Magneto or former New Jersey Mayor Chris Christie.

We are a typically reserved Northwoods people. Even our villains would tend to be low-key and likely to blend in with the crowd, especially if their capes were plaid, but there is one foe that is bigger and badder than all the rest: The Weather.

The Weather is a villain for all seasons, but he really kicks up a fuss in the winter. Our breezes are arctic blasts. Our chills are polar vortexes. Our Easter egg hunts stink because the kids keep bogging down in the snow.

They say you can't change The Weather, but Yooperman would do his best to fight it. First of all, he's so super he majors in journalism in college, then goes on to work undercover as a reporter at his small farming town newspaper, *The Daily Plant It*.

He secretly monitors his foe with one of those weather cubes, the kind with a button on top that you press for up-to-date forecasts for your region. After pulverizing yet another cube due to his super strength, he then politely asks a co-worker what The Weather will bring.

A blizzard is forecast! And it's May!

Before you know it, he's suited up and flying through the air for coffee because not even Yooperman can avoid his turn for the morning coffee run. After he finishes his own Venti Skinny Vanilla Latte, he's off to take on The Weather.

He wields a snow scoop the size of Paul Bunyan's ax, and clears Baraga County before you can say "Pass the road salt." He also plows a path on Keweenaw Bay to 240 feet deep, because I am typing this story and that's where I like to fish.

He takes a mighty breath and blasts the cold air back where it came from, which rubs Canada wrong but endears him to polar bears. Turning his head a neat 180 degrees, he hits his intake button and draws warm air up from the south, finally assuring a Happy Easter for all.

When he's done, Yooperman returns to his office and more important concerns, like senior citizens' cribbage scores and junior high basketball and March is Reading Month, because Yooperman has bills to pay too, you know.

At least until the price of scrap goes up again.

18. REPORTING FOR DUTY

Goodbye, Pulitzer

In direct contrast to my usual flagrant waste of white space, this piece was supposed to be hard hitting, cutting-edge and, do I dare type it out loud? Double dare? PULITZER worthy!

Then my own dad shot me down.

Dad fought all over Europe in WWII. He landed on Normandy Beach. He was in the Battle of the Bulge. He helped liberate France, along with a fair amount of its wine. And almost every week, 146 letters spread out over the years 1942-1945, Dad wrote home to tell about it.

The letters were tied in three bundles and stashed away in a shoe box in my folks' basement. Dad left us in 2000. Mom joined him in 2013. The shoe box has been tucked in a corner of my desk at home ever since, just waiting to be duly recorded.

The thing about duly recording is it takes a lot of typing, so I put it off as long as I could until last weekend brought bad weather and worse TV. They are the very building blocks of Pulitzer-winning stories. It was time to bring Dad's fascinating war years to light.

The letters were mostly in order and written on whatever paper Dad could find. The earliest were on military stationery, some were on notebook pages, others on construction paper and a few on paper thin as tissue. Dad's old familiar handwriting flowed throughout.

About two letters in, I realized something was missing. It was my nomination for a Pulitzer Prize. Instead of giving the full story in riveting detail, Dad spent four years trying to convince his folks that in the midst of war-torn Europe, often fighting on the front line, he was just fine and dandy.

Oct. 11, 1943—I can't tell you the name of the camp but it's a very nice place. The food is good, the weather is fine, and I'm feeling tops.

Feb. 12, 1944—I'm still 100% and everything's going along pretty good. You know I can just imagine how you two must be worrying about my safety over here, so I'm going to tell you again not to. You just remember what I told you both that nite at the depot: that 'I'm coming back' and that's for sure!

My annual reports from Fish Camp (coming soon—hide the children) are more fraught with danger, and the only time we come under fire is when Slick lights up the grill. I've seen "Saving Private Ryan." I knew my dad was there. I gently dug out the letter he sent right after D-day.

June 8, 1944—I suppose all of you at home are pretty much excited about what has taken place over here these past two days. All I can say is that I'm feeling 100%, and don't worry about me cause I'm in a pretty safe spot.

I can't make this a very long letter tonite because I'm really a bit sleepy, in fact I've only had about 8 hrs. snooze these past few days. So believe me, that old sack of mine (even though it's just a blanket roll on the ground) is going to look pretty good tonite. Love & Smooches, Bob.

No zinging of bullets. No gut-wrenching fear. And what was with the Love & Smooches?

That was my dad. He lost only one paragraph to the war, to censors when he described a piece of equipment in too much detail. He wrote four pages about his reunion with his brother, Don, in France. He wrote one sentence telling Ma & Pa he'd received a Presidential Citation.

Must have done something right.

On the lighter side, which Dad would have wanted you to read anyway, he wrote about he and his buddies meeting French girls in clubs. They taught them American slang, then how to cuss, then it all backfired because when the girls got mad, they could tell the American boys exactly how they felt.

He asked Pa to retrieve his high school ring from a former girlfriend. Then he asked him to give it to his current girlfriend. Neither woman was my mother. Now I know why Dad's box of war letters never made it upstairs.

And that was pretty much my dad's war in print. It wasn't about saving the world. It was about sparing his parents, and keeping his promise: 'I'm coming back.'

May 7, 1945—Well it just happened, the last of the German army gave up just a few hours ago, and the war over here is over! Most of the guys were mighty quiet as they heard it, none of us felt too much like doing all the shouting & gun shooting we'd talked about doing when this day did arrive. In fact most of us were doing a lot of sober thinking, thinking of all we'd gone through and of the boys who came over here with us who will never return.

Thank you for your service, Dad. Love & Smooches, Nancy

Lefties Just Aren't Right

Several months ago, an astute reader accused our newspaper editor of being a leftist.

He was so right!

The newspaper I work for is indeed left-wing. Editor Barry Drue is left-handed. Associate Editor Chris Ford is left handed. Reporter Besonen is a lefty. Ad man Joe Schutte is right-handed but fits in so well, he's clearly living in denial.

So long as my desk is within pitching distance of my co-workers, who have sharp pens and are not afraid to throw them, I am not at liberty to comment in print on their leftist ways. Instead, I will attempt to dispel rumors about lefties in general, with a little help from the internet.

We are a fairly exclusive bunch, comprising only about 10 percent of the population. Left-handed men outnumber left-handed women, but only by a little. Contrary to popular opinion, lefties aren't clumsy; we write funny because we're always getting short-chained by businesses that value their pens.

Left-handed play is banned in polo, because polo ponies are trained to expect their riders' mallet to be swung from the right. Left-handed play is also banned in field hockey because people, like ponies, could get hurt.

It is always fun to note famous people who share our lefty ways. Pablo Picasso and Leonardo da Vinci were both left-handed. Marilyn Monroe was, too. President Bill Clinton was a southpaw. President George W. Bush wasn't right, either.

While lefties obviously excel at the arts, presiding, and clocking polo ponies, we too have our crosses to bear. It started in the olden days, when superstitious folks would rap little lefties on the knuckles with a ruler so they would learn to write right.

Now they just hand you your first pair of scissors.

Scissors are a holdover from the olden days, designed by superstitious folks after their rulers were taken away. Scissors fit your right hand like a friendly handshake. Try to cut with your left hand, and you will bore deep grooves into your fingers while spreading the blades apart.

A few years back our youngest, also a lefty, brought home a special pair of scissors from grade school. They had a big L imprinted on their shiny blades. They didn't cut right-handed. They didn't cut left-handed. I think it was one of those life lessons.

You can't go through life resting your writing hand on the spiral in your notebook without becoming a bit calloused. And that is a good thing, because it's easy to feel a bit left out when you're not all right.

I write, shoot arrows, and play pool badly left-handed. In all other sports, I am right-handed. I cut meat with my right hand. Unfortunately, I grasp scissors with my left. At feeding time, again unfortunately, both hands work equally well.

There are a few lefty tests out there, none of them foolproof, but here's just a sampling if you too tend to straddle the fence and want to finally know the truth:

Which hand do you write with?

Do your scissors cut?

Ever hurt a polo pony?

If the answer to all of the above is a resounding "Yes!", then you are a left-winger, too. Grab up a pencil, which doesn't smudge as badly as ink, and circle August 13 on your calendar for International Lefthanders Day, a celebration of folks who just aren't right.

Adding My Two Bits

The newsstand price of the newspaper I work for recently rose 25 cents. I have been living the good life ever since.

Like other members of the nouveau riche, which is French for "got an extra quarter now," I have had to suffer the slings and arrows of those who cannot deal with my wealth. As soon as they spot me cruising through town in my rusty Toyota, my former peers can't help but holler:

"So! Whatcha' doing with ALL THAT MONEY?"

There's no use trying to hide the truth in a small town. Sooner or later it's going to make the rounds at the co-op. With a loud sigh, I instruct my chauffeur, which is French for "my 16-year-old son who just got his license," to pull over so I can set the record straight.

"The villa got a fresh coat of paint," I reply in an appropriately bored manner. "As for the castle in Europe, if you're going to have flying buttresses, darling, you've got to maintain them. And by the way, I no longer shop generic."

Then my chauffeur turns up his Led Zeppelin CD again, and accelerates in a manner that causes me to use language below my newly rich standing. I hardly recover from takeoff when he pulls into the gas station and it starts all over again.

"Are you paying with ALL THOSE QUARTERS?"

Alright then, you wisenheimers, here's the dirt: now that people are paying an extra two bits to read about their children's sports and find out who's in District Court News this week, I have been living the good life in the U.P.

I can buy another t-shirt from the thrift shop two-bits bin. I can afford another pull on the one-armed bandit at the casino. I can indulge in metered parking in town, as long as I don't linger over my two-bit purchases at the thrift shop.

Most people do not go into journalism to get rich. They go into it because they were bad at math, but had no difficulty knocking out a five-page report on *Beowulf*. Truly gifted journalists could accomplish the feat without even reading *Beowulf*.

When typewriters still inhabited the earth, we journalism majors didn't have to re-type our work, or even cover our errors with white-out. We could use editing symbols. Journalists could be bad at both math and typing, and still earn a college degree!

The first hitch was, we had to have ethics. Ethics 101, to be precise. In Ethics, we learned we had to ask the hard questions, be objective, get our facts straight and look up people's names in the phone book so they wouldn't call in complaints after the paper hit the stands.

The second hitch became clear a few months before graduation, at the college's job placement office. That's where we signed up to interview with potential employers like the *Wall Street Journal*, or our second pick, the *Illinois Rockford Register Star*.

It soon became apparent that if your degree included the words "business" or "computers," even if they were slightly misspelled, the world was your oyster. Major corporations couldn't get enough of you, especially if the writing on your t-shirt was in Greek.

If you had ink on your fingers and could spell "Beowulf," nobody wanted to talk to you.

As commencement neared and I realized my phone was still not ringing, I re-visited the office to remind the staff of my pending unemployment. I got instant results.

"Oh. You want to work for a newspaper. You got a bicycle?"

Because we're in the business of asking the hard questions, we can't blame our readers for grilling us about pulling in more money. The truth is, that extra quarter is simply paying for higher production and insurance costs.

I got my new bicycle bell from the two-bits bin at the thrift shop.

Writing in My Sleep

Good morning. The subject of today's rather one-sided discussion is sleep deprivation.

Like Americans across America, my light tends to shine brightest well after the cows come home. According to a sleep deprivation specialist, my daughter who has three small children that all sleep in shifts, it starts in the womb.

I am comfortable sharing this in print because she's too tired to read it. If you call her to rat me out, the six-year-old will pick up and chat about her school day, while the four- and two-year-olds fight for their turn to talk.

And she will gladly let them do it, especially if it's me calling again, because she is very pregnant with our newest lovely grandchild. She literally hasn't slept in years, because sleep deprivation begins before birth.

Babies love to be rocked to sleep. Pregnant moms rock their inner babies all day long, while they are cooking and cleaning and picking up after their other children who are fighting to talk to whoever is on the phone.

When pregnant mothers finally lie down at night, their inner babies hit the dance floor. They rock and roll and aim high kicks at their mothers' bladders until it's time for their mothers to get up again and rock them back to sleep.

Most children continue the pattern until their teens, when they awaken only for louder music, food, and texting. This is just fine with their parents, because it lets them catch a few winks before their own inner clock starts ringing off the shelf, reminding them their time is running out and they're wasting it in the sack.

I like to lay the blame for my sleep-free nights on our own three children, my husband's years of working swing shift, and Bob the cat, who used to wake me up every night so she could use her woodland restroom.

I have always been the victim, and that's worked out just fine by me, because most of my work is done in the wee hours. The TV is off, the moon is up, and my kids are up, too, but now it's with their kids in their own homes. Settled into a comfy corner of the couch with my laptop, I can finally focus on my writing.

Then the second shift begins.

My husband can't sleep very well, either, because he napped in his chair earlier in the day and I'm typing too loudly. He gets up, so I go back to bed. Then he comes back to bed, which wakes me up again. I get up, grab my laptop, and head for the couch where I continue typing, loudly.

Sometime between 5 and 8 a.m. we are both up for the day, and I'm sending in another column to the newspaper. Sometimes readers will ask me, from a safe distance of course, how I come up with ideas for my column.

I'd have to say they started in the womb.

J-Grad vs. Evolution

Technically speaking, everything I learned in college is obsolete.

As educators everywhere loudly harrumph in a unified act of harrumphing, allow me to explain. I went to college. I learned how to put together a newspaper, with some life skills, such as "don't close the Red Lion Inn on school nights," thrown in.

Then they all got obsolete.

I still don't close the Red Lion Inn on school nights, mostly because it's now a 400-mile commute. However, most of what I learned in J-school, which is geeky shop talk for college of journalism, pretty much belongs on a stone tablet held aloft by Charlton Heston.

No, I did not go to college with him. Go Google him already.

J-school taught many important rules I still strictly adhere to. I check my facts. I hold my first paragraph to 20 words or less. I write to the seventh-grade level, just as my instructors instructed. I probably shouldn't have shared that.

A good J-grad should also meet deadlines and use proper grammar. Most of all, she should be absolutely objective in her writing, no matter which side of Keweenaw Bay she lives on, as in, "Go L'Anse Hornets! Go Baraga Vikings, too!"

The rules of responsible writing still stand. I just choose to break them in my weekly columns, which are always surrounded by a solid black line to prevent bad grammar seepage. It is the technical side of my education that has been kicked to the curb, or as they now say in the biz, "deleted."

Take typing. It was an early form of keyboarding that involved ink ribbons, sheets of paper, and a metal bar you'd smartly whack to start every new line. As a dedicated J-student, I would haul out my blue portable typewriter just before deadline and pound out my story. Then I would cut, rearrange, and glue it all back together, resulting in either good news or bad art.

When I wasn't busy gluing together stories, I was spending many a happy hour cooped up in the darkroom, where I developed and printed stunning images I'd captured all over DeKalb, IL. Mostly, corn and cows.

We learned how to mix chemicals, thread film onto metal reels in pitch darkness, develop our film, and print the images on photo paper. As a matter of fact, my first job offer was Darkroom Manager for a newspaper in Libertyville, IL. They must have liked my Herefords.

I am so glad I chose to go toward the light, even if my writing has to be boxed-in to protect the reading public. Reporting has allowed me to use all my hard-earned skills, including one that has no practical application whatsoever anymore unless I get a job in a J-museum: newspaper layout.

The layout process used to involve sharp scissors and hot wax. Also a lot of long, boring strips of copy, but I was going for edgy here because J-anything is not terribly dangerous work. The wax wasn't even all that hot. Sometimes we ran with our scissors, but nobody ever fell.

Instead, it was the dawn of the Computer Age that nearly wiped us off the face of the earth.

Nobody heard it coming because our typewriters were really noisy. It somehow sneaked up the stairs and into our composition room, where there was much rejoicing because computers really did make the job a lot easier for the ladies in composition.

Then Diane, who was computing all my layout for me, took away my scissors.

I've been walking and working upright ever since, though I still slip and use the word "film" sometimes when referring to digital camera images. This makes the other cavemen I work with guffaw loudly and scratch their heads at a dim yet fond memory.

Because there are no J-rules on being objective about your fellow reporters.

About the author

Nancy Besonen was born and raised on Chicago's South Side. Her interest in writing and fishing landed her in Michigan's Upper Peninsula where she enjoyed a 30-year career as a reporter for the *L'Anse Sentinel*. Her weekly humor column, Off the Hook, always aimed at keeping it light, from Fitting in at FinnFest to being a Bad Woman in the Woods to taking her crowbar to court, in Besonen vs. Crowbar, for a bad rap. Whether (figuratively) vying for the title of Mrs. U.P. in a gown fashioned from glittering canning lids, or facing down a wolf with a loaded paintbrush (for real), Besonen celebrates every aspect of Northwoods living and beyond. She and her husband, Don, have three children and a small herd of grandchildren, all delightfully near, who provide love, laughter, and abundant inspiration.